Praise for

The Essence of Joy

The **Essence of Joy** touched my heart with its compelling stories of forgiveness woven against the backdrop of the aromas mentioned throughout the Bible – frankincense, myrrh, cedarwood, cinnamon...

~~Patricia Bradley, Award-winning author, the **Logan Point Series** and the **Memphis Cold Case** novels

A Must Read! In **The Essence of Joy**, Lynn Watson intertwines Scripture with the uses of oils and spices mentioned in the Bible. I was left with a feeling of wonder, a new way of looking at God's word. The book is educational, entertaining, and uplifting. There's history, fun-facts, even recipes. The author brings devotionals to a new level, giving biblical insight to the problems modern women encounter today.

The Essence of Joy is perfect for both bible study groups and those who are just starting out on their spiritual journey.

~~Jeri McBryde, Eight-Time Contributing Author to **Chicken Soup for the Soul**

It's fascinating to follow how fragrances and spices were used in the Bible. These will have more meaning to me now. Some of these verses I've read time after time and haven't noticed the connections. The simple traditions we take part in have so much history that I didn't know.

~~Rhonda Moody, Women's Ministry Associate, First West Church, West Monroe, LA

The Essence of Joy utilizes all five senses to bring the truths of God's word to life. Watson weaves relatable stories that would appeal to the inexperienced Bible reader as well as life-long Christians. She reveals lesser known facts about Biblical scents that will enrich your study of the Bible. Great Read!!

~~Michelle Hammons, former Chairman Children's Ministry Committee at Second Presbyterian Church (Memphis, TN), Bible Study Fellowship Small Group Leader, and Happy Christian Woman

Inspirational Collection for Women, Volume 2

The Essence of Joy

Filling Your Heart with the Aromas of Jesus' Nativity

Lynn U. Watson

Cover Illustration by Allisha Mokry

Unless otherwise noted, all Scripture quotations are taken from the Holman Christian Standard Bible®, Copyright ® 1999, 2000, 2002, 2003, 2009 by Holman Bible Publishers. Used by permission. Holman Christian Standard Bible®, Holman CSB®, and HCSB® are federally registered trademarks of Holman Bible Publishers.

Other Bible Versions quoted:

Scripture quotations taken from the New American Standard Bible® (NASB), Copyright © 1960, 1962, 1963, 1968, 1971, 1972, 1973, 1975, 1977, 1995 by The Lockman Foundation Used by permission. www.Lockman.org

Scripture quotations marked (NIV) are taken from **THE HOLY BIBLE, NEW INTERNATIONAL VERSION®, NIV®. Copyright © 1973, 1978, 1984, 2011 by Biblica, Inc.™ Used by permission. All rights reserved worldwide.**

Scripture quotations marked (NLT) are taken from the Holy Bible, New Living Translation, copyright © 1996, 2004, 2007 by Tyndale House Foundation. Used by permission of Tyndale House Publishers, Inc., Carol Stream, Illinois 60188. All rights reserved.

Scripture quotations marked (The Message) taken from **The Message**. Copyright © 1993, 1994, 1995, 1996, 2000, 2001, 2002. Used by permission of NavPress Publishing Group.

Scripture quotations marked (RSV) are from Revised Standard Version of the Bible, copyright © 1946, 1952, and 1971 National Council of the Churches of Christ in the United States of America. Used by permission. All rights reserved worldwide.

Scripture quotations marked (TLB) are from The Living Bible copyright © 1971 by Tyndale House Foundation. Used by permission of Tyndale House Publishers Inc., Carol Stream, Illinois 60188. All rights reserved. The Living Bible, TLB, and the The Living Bible logo are registered trademarks of Tyndale House Publishers.

Scripture quotations marked (TLV) are from Tree of Life (TLV) Translation of the Bible. Copyright © 2015 by The Messianic Jewish Family Bible Society.

Scriptures marked (VOICE) are taken from The Voice™. Copyright © 2008 by Ecclesia Bible Society. Used by permission. All rights reserved.

Scripture quotations taken from the Amplified® Bible (AMP). Copyright © 2015 by The Lockman Foundation Used by permission. www.Lockman.org

©Copyright 2017, Lynn U. Watson
All rights reserved.
ISBN: 978-0-692-96391-3

As the hand is made for holding and the eye for seeing,
You have fashioned me for joy.
Share with me the vision that shall find it everywhere:
in the violet's beauty;
in the lark's melody;
in the face of a steadfast man;
in a child's smile;
in a mother's love;
in the purity of Jesus.

~~Gaelic Prayer

---

[1] John Philip Newell (commentary); Mary C. Earle (annotation); prayer translation by Alistair MacLean, *Celtic Christian Spirituality: Essential Writings Annotated and Explained,* (Woodstock, Vermont: SkyLight Paths Publishing, 2011), page 59

Contents

Introduction
A Letter to the Reader 13
A Few Hints for Using this Inspirational Volume 14

Chapter 1: Myrrh/The Joy of Abiding 17
Chapter 2: Cedarwood/The Joy of Protection 39
Chapter 3: Frankincense/The Joy of Forgiveness 53
Chapter 4: Rose/The Joy of Love 71
Chapter 5: Mint/The Joy of Giving 89
Chapter 6: Fig/The Joy of Security 103
Chapter 7: Cinnamon/The Joy of Integrity 119
Chapter 8: Citron/The Joy of Legacy 135
Chapter 9: Palm/The Joy of Celebration 155

Before You Go... 171
A Few Parting Thoughts 173
Cinnamah Brosia's Profile 176
Resources 186
Disclaimers 187
Acknowledgements 188
Dear Friends 190

Introduction

Thank you for taking the time to read the introduction.
You'll be really glad you did, because it contains
important information for my inspirational
collection to make sense.

--Cinnamah-Brosia

Dear Friend,

    Smells of sheep, donkeys, oxen, and other animals filled the stable in Bethlehem that special night so long ago. Barnyard perfumes invaded His nostrils as the infant, Jesus, entered our world. First century women regularly used aromatic creams and lotions. Those Mary likely carried in her luggage would have covered the inevitable barnyard stenches.

    Today anticipation of Christmas celebrations evokes thoughts of our favorite seasonal scents. The wise men brought Jesus frankincense and myrrh. Other aromas like cedarwood and cinnamon waft through the pages of Scripture. Volume 2 of my inspirational collection for women tarries at locations in the Bible filled with the scents we love. Be amazed at how many of the season's must-have aromas are captured in the Bible's pages. In ***The Essence of Joy*** we connected them to the manger's star – Jesus Himself – the magnificent gift of our Daddy God* to us, His children.

    My friends and I share life lessons and experiences, emphasizing symbolism and attributes of each essential oil, spice, fruit, or plant featured in this volume, followed by an up close look at them in Scripture. We visit women of the Bible who experience the essence of these spices and fruits through lessons they learned, too. Icing on the cake comes in the form of Essence Droplets – "Fun Facts" and "Your Turn" – providing hands-on opportunities for you to make them more relevant in your life.

    I pray you experience a joyous Christmas season, your heart filled with the aromas of Jesus' nativity.

I love you in Jesus, my precious friend,

Cinnamah-Brosia

---

*Daddy is the literal translation of the name Abba appearing often in the Bible.

A Few Hints for Using this Inspirational Volume

1. Cinnamah-Brosia and Friends Share Their Stories: These fictional characters introduce us to favorite fruits and aromas of the Christmas season, sharing their own stories about the essence in their lives. *(All the stories in the "Cinnamah-Brosia and Friends Share Their Stories" sections are based on events shared by real flesh and blood women. The stories have been fictionalized to fit our characters and timelines appropriately as well as to protect actual identities.)* They prepare us to discover the essence in Scripture and to meet a woman of the Bible whose own life exemplifies its attributes. "C-B" loves essential oils, baking, music, and God's Word. She spreads that love around. In these sections you will become better acquainted with her, learn what she's diffusing, and discover the café's special of the day, a song that's playing, and the Scripture verse she's posted. *(The oils chosen for diffusing may not be the same one featured for that fruit or spice, but they are ones typically readily available and complement the essence for that selection. Songs playing are an eclectic variety of old and new – mostly Christmas – songs. We hope you know and love many, and others will become new favorites. Just like "what's diffusing," each song was chosen to complement the subject matter.)*

2. The Essence in Scripture: a devotion that speaks of the fruit, spice or oil in context of Scripture. All personal stories included in "The Essence in Scripture" sections are drawn from the author's own experiences.

3. A Woman of the Bible Experiences the Essence: a devotion featuring a woman of the Bible who experiences some aspect of that essence in her life. All personal stories included in "A Woman of the Bible Experiences the Essence of" sections are drawn from the author's own experiences.

4. Essence Droplets: a collection of "Fun Facts" about each fruit, oil or spice; and "Your Turn" provides practical ways for you to incorporate them into your world.

Residing between the lines of Bible stories are real people like you and me. Consideration was made regarding how their lives may have been impacted by their culture and how they may have interacted with each other. Certainly, details may have been different than depicted, but the ones shared are definitely plausible. There's something to learn from each one. You may see each person in a different light than the picture you have in mind. We see each other in different lights, too. Thank you, Heavenly Father, You see us through the Light of Jesus.

Many of the characters in the Cinnamah-Brosia stories were introduced in the first volume of this collection, ***The Essence of Courage.*** For your convenience we've included a profile of Cinnamah-Brosia, a cast of characters in the order you first meet them in the book, and an article providing a more detailed picture of The Coffee Cottage.

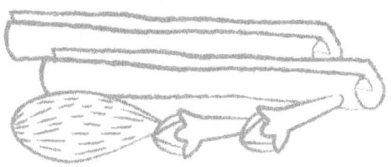

Chapter 1

Myrrh
The Joy of Abiding

Cinnamah-Brosia and Friends share about
Myrrh – The Joy of Abiding

Diffusing Today: Myrrh, Nutmeg & Tangerine
Aromatic Influence: May help create an uplifting yet calming environment
Special of the Day: Hot Chocolate Coffee
Musically: **Breath of Heaven** (Amy Grant)
Verse of the Day:

Abide in Me, and I in you.
As the branch cannot bear fruit of itself unless it abides in the vine, so neither can you unless you abide in Me.
~John 15:4 (NASB)

"C-B, what terrified me so much about this trip? Do you remember?" Haley burst through the door, her eyes sparkling like stars, smile as broad as the sky, and whole paragraphs spilling out faster than gushing rapids.

Haley's passion announces her visit — every time. Today's expressions promised a mountain top story, so unlike the one that tumbled from her anguished heart a year ago. She and Dan had plummeted to depths of despair with overwhelming health and career challenges. Friends intervened with the love of Jesus, through practical help and support.

Transformation for their family abundantly blossomed since that dreadful day. Life's demands with careers, an active first grader, and a baby on the way provided ample opportunities for creatively juggling schedules and responsibilities.

Thriving in her role in the social media world, her boss asked Haley to attend a conference half way across the continent. While honored by the opportunity, she knew she would travel solo, leaving her family behind for several days. She created a million impossible reasons to decline. Our women's small group led her to a place of calm. Together we spawned a plan for Dan and Jaxon during her four-day absence. We prayed over Haley, and for her and the family while she was away, reminding her the enemy produced the irrational thoughts fueling her fears.

> *You see, God did not give us a cowardly spirit*
> *but, a powerful, loving, and disciplined spirit.*
> ~2 Timothy 1:7 (VOICE)

By all appearances today, the trip registered as an out-of-this world experience. "I learned so many things, C-B. I met awesome people. They invited me to dinner with them at a special restaurant that night, but you know me. Uncomfortable in the unfamiliar setting, I excused myself from the group. Then uncertainty about the next couple unscheduled hours smothered me. I recalled the words and prayers of our precious group here at The Coffee Cottage.

"The mall adjacent to the conference hotel bustled with activity. Why I chose to enter a setting that so quickly unnerves me remains beyond my understanding. But know what?! I wandered through the stores and shops and stopped for a snack. A few purchases for the children later, I returned to the hotel. Along the way I pondered the experience. I know He wasn't physically with me, but I felt like Jesus had been right by my side the whole time. It was as though He had chatted and laughed with me. I felt His delight at the joy of children on the playground. I believe as I shopped He smiled at my 'finds.' I sang praise songs all the way back to the hotel. If anyone heard, I never noticed.

"Alone in my bed that night, I thanked Him for the opportunity to absorb so many new ideas to help our clients and for faithful friends at home that made the time away possible. I thanked Him for Dan who proved to be far more capable with the children than I often give him credit. I offered yet another prayer of thanks for the generosity and trust of my boss. Most of all I thanked Him for this precious time in His presence. I pondered every moment. The intensity of realizing how much He loved me and cared for me overwhelmed my human mind and heart. It also filled me with an unexplainable joy! I attempted to picture Mary holding Baby Jesus and 'pondering all these things in her heart.' Pure Inexpressible Joy!"

Cinnamah found herself near speechless. Haley had shared a most intimate moment. A deep breath or two later C-B responded. "Wow! Haley, I would have totally understood had you chosen to keep this encounter with Jesus private. I'm so touched you shared it with me. I'm incredibly blessed by this beautiful encouragement. My heart sings with yours."

Haley encountered Jesus in a most dramatic way. Have you experienced a significant adventure with Jesus that causes you to ponder as she did? For many of us there are shorter, but equally tender moments — glimpses even — abiding with Him in such intimacy. Maybe you relate more that way.

For Haley, these were moments of intimate worship and reverence. We meet Jesus in amazing ways when we choose to spend time with Him. In their book, Sitting at the Feet of Rabbi Jesus, Anne Spangler and Lois Tverberg ask:

> *"Would it surprise you to learn that the rabbis thought study and not prayer, was the highest form of worship? They pointed out when we pray, we speak to God, but when we study the Scriptures, God speaks to us. Of course, they weren't advocating a coldly intellectual approach to Scripture, but the kind of study that is motivated by a deep reverence for God's Word."*[2]

Haley's intimate encounter with Jesus emanated from the love relationship she faithfully cultivated with Him in His Word – the first place to look to experience cherished moments with Him. We may or may not receive the opportunity she did. None of us will experience the kind of intimacy Mary did at Jesus' birth. (We'll spend time with her as our woman of the Bible for myrrh.) But abiding in His Word allows the Holy Spirit to touch our hearts and spirits, assuring us of Jesus nearness. Will you abide with Him

---

[2] Anne Spangler and Lois Tverberg, *Sitting at the Feet of Rabbi Jesus*, (Grand Rapids, Michigan: Zondervan, 2009) page 26.

today? He speaks to us through Scripture as surely as He did to Haley in the mall.

> *When the Spirit of truth comes, he will guide you into all truth. He will not speak on his own but will tell you what he has heard. He will tell you about the future. He will bring me glory by telling you whatever he receives from me. All that belongs to the Father is mine; this is why I said, 'The Spirit will tell you whatever he receives from me.*
>
> ~John 16:13-15 (NLT)

The Essence of Myrrh in Scripture
Follow the Myrrh Markers

Part 1 – Old Testament
From Joseph and the Ishmaelite Traders to Solomon's Bride

Botanical Name: Commiphora myrrha;
oil steam-distilled from gum resin;
native to the Southwest Arabian Peninsula and Ethiopia

Car tank's full. Hop in, my friend, buckle up, and let's go road tripping. Destination: the beach. Lying in the sun with a good book is almost heaven. Today's book: The Good Book, features a trail of myrrh meandering its pages from Genesis to Revelation -- from the Spice Route to the Crystal Sea. So many "Myrrh Markers" attract attention along the way creating a fascinating treasure map. Let the journey begin!

God promised the elderly Abraham one day his offspring would be as numerous as the stars in the sky. Abraham's wife laughed at the thought. After all, her age and stage of life far surpassed the norm for childbearing. The One True Living God orchestrated one miracle following another that carried us down an amazing road.

In their old age Sarah conceived and gave birth to a bouncing baby boy, Isaac. God called upon Abraham to sacrifice his son, tying him to an altar and burning him. Savage as this act sounds, Abraham obeyed and trusted God. In the nick of time God provided a ram as a substitute. Isaac's life continued with unimaginable twists and turns. Isaac fathered Jacob and Esau. Twelve sons carry Jacob's name. Jacob (not his wife) stitched a multi-colored coat for Joseph, his favorite. Count on it. More favoritism followed. Joseph threw that in his brothers' faces a time or two or three. Their disrespect for him grew as tall as the fairytale beanstalk. You may read the whole story of Abraham and his growing family beginning in Genesis 11.

Watch for our first mile marker, the first mention of myrrh in the Bible, in Genesis 37. Myrrh's serious staying power gives it prominent position in the perfume industry as a fixative for other fragrances. The Bible tracks myrrh with serious staying power as well, abiding from coast to coast in The Good Book. Let's make our first stop on our way to the beach.

Myrrh Marker #1:

Abraham and Sarah's great grandsons often ganged up on their brother, Joseph. This particular time in Dothan Judah played instigator. He and the brothers sold Joseph as a slave to Ishmaelite traders. They carried costly spices, including myrrh, from Gilead to Egypt.

> *Then they sat down to eat their meal. As they did, they saw some Ishmaelite traders coming from Gilead. Their camels were loaded with spices, lotion and myrrh. They were on their way to take them down to Egypt. Judah said to his brothers, "What will we gain if we kill our brother and try to cover up what we've done?*
> ~Genesis 37:25-26 (NIV)

After splashing Joseph's colorful coat with animal blood the boys returned it to their dad. Assuming the worst, Jacob mourned the death of his favorite son.

Myrrh Marker #2:

Potiphar, Captain of the Palace Guard, purchased Joseph from the traders upon their arrival in Egypt. For 20 years Joseph gained great favor and ascended to high office in Egypt, until the trickery of Potiphar's manipulative wife landed him in prison. Interestingly, the prison guards showed him favor, as well. While imprisoned he gained a reputation for interpreting dreams.

Pharaoh sought Joseph's insight for his troubling dreams. God led Joseph to share: seven years of plenty and feasting would end in seven years of severe famine. The answer impressed Pharaoh, and he restored Joseph's palace influence. Ultimately, what the brothers intended for evil, resulted in a grand family reunion.

Suffering from famine in the land, many years later Jacob sent the boys to Egypt praying they could find help and food there. Jacob loaded the group up with quality gifts to gain favor for his family, unaware he again honored his favorite son.

> *Then their father Israel said to them, 'If it must be, then do this: put some of the best products of the land in your bags and take them down to the man as a gift – a little balm and a little honey, some spices and myrrh, some pistachio nuts and almonds.*
>
> ~Genesis 43:11 (NIV)

Myrrh Marker #3

Joseph settled his dad, brothers and their families in Egypt. Following Joseph's death, the growing nation worked as slaves. In spite of harsh conditions, the people thrived for generation upon generation. Centuries later, the sitting Pharaoh dictated all the male Israelite babies be aborted at birth by the attending midwives. Baby Moses escaped when his mom and sister placed him in a reed basket and set him afloat on the Nile River. Adoption by the Pharaoh's daughter followed. As an adult, God chose Moses to lead his nation's exodus to God's Promised Land.

During forty years of wilderness wanderings, Moses received revelations and instructions from God that became the heart of restoration and worship for God's people. The rituals foreshadowed the coming Messiah's sacrifice for all who choose to follow Him. Two fragrant recipes waft from those instructions. Both the holy anointing oil and the incense included myrrh. Incense required stacte — myrrh in its purest form.

> *Then the Lord said to Moses, "Take the following fine spices: 500 shekels of liquid myrrh, half as much (that is, 250 shekels) of fragrant cinnamon, 250 shekels of fragrant*

calamus, 500 shekels of cassia—all according to the sanctuary shekel—and a hin of olive oil. Make these into a sacred anointing oil, a fragrant blend, the work of a perfumer. It will be the sacred anointing oil.
~Exodus 30:23-25 (NIV)

The Lord said to Moses: "Take fragrant spices: stacte, onycha, and galbanum; the spices and pure frankincense are to be in equal measures. Prepare expertly blended incense from these; it is to be seasoned with salt, pure and holy. Grind some of it into a fine powder and put some in front of the testimony in the tent of meeting, where I will meet with you. It must be especially holy to you. As for the incense you are making, you must not make any for yourselves using its formula. It is to be regarded by you as sacred to the Lord. Anyone who makes something like it to smell its fragrance must be cut off from his people."
~Exodus 30:34-38

Myrrh Marker #4

King Ahasuerus of Persia hosted a beauty pageant to find a new queen. Her cousin Mordecai entered the young Jewish woman into the contest. She won! As queen, Esther saved God's people from annihilation. God chose her "for such a time as this." Through her actions, His abiding love continued to surround His children. Esther's beauty preparations before meeting with her husband, the king, included myrrh baths. Her story occupies one whole book of the Bible: Esther. Be sure to read it there. You'll also find Queen Esther's story in *The Essence of Courage*.

During the year before each young woman's turn to go to King Ahasuerus, the harem regulation required her to receive beauty treatments with oil of myrrh for six months

---

[3]Lynn U. Watson, *The Essence of Courage: Cultivating the Fruit of the Spirit in Solomon's Locked Garden and in Your Heart*, (Bartlett, Tennessee: Lynn U. Watson, 2016) pages 101-104.

and then with perfumes and cosmetics for another six months.

~Esther 2:12

If you keep silent at this time, liberation and deliverance will come to the Jewish people from another place, but you and your father's house will be destroyed. Who knows, perhaps you have come to your royal position for such a time as this."

~Esther 4:14

Myrrh Marker #5

Journeying on we hear a royal wedding song coming from the sons of Korah. Psalm 45 fills our senses with prophetic imagery of the coming Messiah, our ultimate bridegroom. Of course, if myrrh saturates every sacrifice, Jesus garments carry the aroma, too.

You love righteousness and hate wickedness; therefore God, your God, has anointed you with the oil of joy more than your companions. Myrrh, aloes, and cassia perfume all your garments; from ivory palaces harps bring you joy. Kings' daughters are among your honored women; the queen, adorned with gold from Ophir, stands at your right hand.

~Psalm 45:7-9

Myrrh Marker #6

Solomon described his bride in aromatic images of spices and essential oils. He honored her gentleness (a gift of the Holy Spirit) as myrrh.

In the book of Proverbs, Solomon also acknowledges the dangerous allure of myrrh when the temptress employs its cunning aromas. Proverbs 7 warns of prostitutes who allure from the street

---

[4]Lynn U. Watson, *The Essence of Courage: Cultivating the Fruit of the Spirit in Solomon's Locked Garden and in Your Heart*, (Bartlett, Tennessee: Lynn U. Watson, 2016), Chapter 8, pages 145-159.

corner beckoning men into dangerous territory. Myrrh nestles itself among the tools of her trade.

> *"I've perfumed my bed with myrrh, aloes, and cinnamon. Come, let's drink deeply of lovemaking until morning. Let's feast on each other's love! My husband isn't home; he went on a long journey. He took a bag of money with him and will come home at the time of the full moon." She seduces him with her persistent pleading; she lures with her flattering talk.*
> ~Proverbs 7:17-21

Follow the Myrrh Markers

Part 2 – New Testament
From the Kings Bearing Gifts for the Baby to the Crystal Sea

Myrrh Marker #7

Turn to follow the royal entourage into the New Testament. Kings of the Orient travel with their train of camels and servants bearing gifts to a newborn King. Among the first baby gifts the family receives, gold, frankincense, and, myrrh are singled out! The kings present them as an act of worship. They've abided in the aroma of myrrh on their extended travels to visit Jesus. God rewards their faithfulness by allowing them to abide in the presence of the King of Kings.

> *Then the star appeared again, the same star they had seen in the eastern skies. It led them on until it hovered over the place of the child. They could hardly contain themselves: They were in the right place! They had arrived at the right time! They entered the house and saw the child in the arms of Mary, his mother. Overcome, they kneeled and worshiped him. Then they opened their luggage and presented gifts: gold, frankincense, myrrh.*
> ~Matthew 2:10-11 (The Message)

Myrrh Marker #8

At His crucifixion, soldiers offered Jesus myrrh mixed with wine to ease His pain. Associated so closely with time at His mother's side, the aroma alone provided comfort and may explain why He refused the drink.

> *And they brought Jesus to the place called Golgotha (which means Skull Place). They tried to give Him wine mixed with myrrh, but He did not take it. Then they crucified Him and divided His clothes, casting lots for them to decide what each would get. Now it was nine in the morning when they crucified Him. The*

inscription of the charge written against Him was: THE KING OF THE JEWS.
                                      ~Mark 15:22-26

Myrrh Marker #9

Determined to learn the truth about this man, Nicodemus, a synagogue ruler, secretly and by cover of night sought out Jesus. Their conversation resulted in the most beloved Bible verse and promise of Jesus — ever

> *For God so loved the world that he gave his one and only Son, that whoever believes in him shall not perish but have eternal life.*
>   ~John 3:16 (NIV)

To honor his love for Jesus, Nicodemus brought abundant treasures of aloes and myrrh to wrap Jesus' body for burial.

> *Later, Joseph of Arimathea asked Pilate for the body of Jesus. Now Joseph was a disciple of Jesus, but secretly because he feared the Jewish leaders. With Pilate's permission, he came and took the body away. He was accompanied by Nicodemus, the man who earlier visited Jesus at night. Nicodemus brought a mixture of myrrh and aloes, about seventy-five pounds. The two of them wrapped Jesus' with strips of linen infused with the spices. This was in accordance with Jewish burial customs.*
>   ~John 19:38-40 (NIV)

Myrrh Marker #10

Along with prayers of God's people, incense (which by God's design, contains myrrh) continuously rises to the throne of God. Billows of myrrh's aroma surround The Father and Jesus reigning together. When Jesus returns for His bride, will we recognize His fragrance before we see His face?

> *Another angel, who had a golden censer, came and stood at the altar. He was given much incense to offer, with the prayers of all God's people, on the golden altar in front of the throne. The smoke of the incense, together with the prayers of God's people, went up before God from the angel's hand.*
> ~Revelation 8:3,4 (NIV)

Precious myrrh abides with us throughout the Bible. The links between these stories provide details of God's plan of salvation put in motion at the beginning of time. The characters on the stage of our journey interconnect to bring us our beloved Redeemer and Friend, Jesus. Our story culminates in the ultimate and joy-filled Holy Beach Party around the Crystal Sea.

What abides in your heart? What do you ponder? Does it bring you joy? The Bible warns us against anger abiding there:

> *Don't let your spirit rush to be angry, for anger abides in the heart of fools.*
> ~Ecclesiastes 7:9

Instead, the author of Psalm 119 spends 176 verses praising God's Word and reasons to keep His Words in our heart. He requests of God:

> *Help me understand the meaning of Your precepts so that I can meditate on Your wonders.*
> ~Psalm 119:27

Make time to read the whole Psalm. It contains many verses, but is only four pages in my Bible. Would you share with us what joys about His Word God impressed upon your heart? We would love for you to post your thoughts on our Facebook page.

NOTE: I read a sermon by C.H. Spurgeon entitled, *A Bundle of Myrrh,* from February 28, 1864, that I found quite inspiring as I wrote about myrrh. You may find it online at: http://www.biblebb.com/files/spurgeon/0558.htm (accessed 9/23/2017)

A Woman of the Bible Experiences the Joy of Abiding
Tender Joy Abiding in Mary's Arms and in Her Heart

Joy emanates out of the abiding sense of God's fierce love for us.[5]
~Margaret Feinberg

Her king, her love, her delight abiding between her breasts and tucked close to her heart, Solomon's bride likens him to a bundle of myrrh.

My love is a sachet of myrrh to me,
spending the night between my breasts.
~Song of Solomon 1:13

We've considered myrrh's importance as a fixative in the perfume industry. Worth noting, in the verse immediately preceding this one, she regarded her lover as perfume.

"While the king was at his table, My perfume (Solomon)
sent forth [his] fragrance [surrounding me].
~Song of Solomon 1:12 (AMP)

Picture the believer abiding in God's Word, holding His every loving kindness close to her heart, and abiding in all she knows of Him. She ponders the immeasurable beauty of His life in hers, humbled and facedown in awe of God's ways so beyond her own. Myrrh releases its fragrance in those tender moments. Because of its staying power, she carries the fragrance of Jesus with her

---

[5] Margaret Feinberg, *Fight Back with Joy: Celebrate More, Regret Less, Stare Down Your Greatest Fears,* (Nashville, Tennessee: LifeWay Press, 2014) page 15. Reprinted and used by permission.

wherever she goes. She recognizes His unstoppable love for her, and joy spills over.

Mary nestled Jesus between her breasts. That's what the mother of a newborn does. I recognize Jesus entered this world in a barn — definitely not a place perfumed with the fresh smell of baby lotion we're accustomed to. However, as women we know she likely packed some sweet smelling lotions and cosmetics for herself and her infant son. As soon as Jesus was born, wise men from the East began preparations for their gift-bearing journey, but their arrival with the myrrh remained several months away.

> *They hurried off and found both Mary and Joseph, and the baby who was lying in the feeding trough. After seeing them, they reported the message they were told about this child, and all who heard it were amazed at what the shepherds said to them. But Mary was treasuring up all these things in her heart and meditating on them.*
> ~Luke 2:16-19

Picture Joseph wrapping a warm shawl around her arms to fend off the late night chill, and notice the innkeeper bringing them hot tea. Cozy and head-over-heels in love with her infant Son, Mary cradles Jesus and rocks Him in her arms. She remembered the visit of the angel. Here in a stable she is surrounded by the unfolding story. Shepherds proclaiming they received the announcement from an angel came to visit her new baby. Mary pondered all that had been and all she could imagine of the future for her child. Consider the thoughts that may have slipped silently into her mind and heart.

- "An angel announced His birth. What will His life be like? What will our life be like?"
- "Just three months along with this pregnancy, baby John jumped for joy in His mother's womb when we arrived at their home. Elizabeth recognized me as the mother of her Lord. How did they even know?"

- "Joseph and I made a tough, but required, journey getting to Bethlehem. My baby came into this world in a barn. I had different plans. This will be quite a birth story to share back home in Nazareth."
- "Then God sent shepherds to visit us. They said angels lit up the sky and sang to them. I know God is in this, but will I ever remember all the things happening to write them in His baby book?"
- "Isn't He the most beautiful baby ever – He's so perfect in every way. Just look at those tiny fingers and toes. What does it really mean that He's the Messiah?"
- "I love this little guy way more than my life. Will He always love His mommy?"

What other thoughts do you imagine Mary had? Whatever they were, it is evident Mary spent many intimate hours abiding with the baby who is our Savior. While no other human is privileged to the moments of mother-son intimacy they shared, Jesus desires a closely bound relationship with each of us.

Have you allowed Jesus to infuse your heart to overflowing with His love? Mary may have believed she was most unworthy of the honor of bearing God's Son, but she treasured the blessings. You may feel you are far too broken to approach Jesus. Fear of His rejection may be hampering your relationship with Him. You may be attending church, but feel removed from His presence.

He was a perfect gift to His mother, Mary. He is the perfect gift for us. He has prepared amazing experiences for the two of you, and He awaits your time together. One visit, and we believe the joy you experience abiding with Him, will call you back again and again.

Going through the motions doesn't please you,
a flawless performance is nothing to you.
I learned God-worship
when my pride was shattered.
Heart-shattered lives ready for love

don't for a moment escape God's notice.
~Psalm 51:16-17 (The Message)

Playing church never delivers the intimacy like a broken life laying hold of His heart and surrendering totally to the Master Fixer. Yes, He does fix us. He fixes us for eternity abiding with Him. Fix, fixative, abiding. Just like myrrh!

Myrrh Essence Droplets

*Surprise us with love at daybreak;
then we'll skip and dance all the day long.*
~Psalm 90:14 (The Message)

Fun Facts:

- Myrrh shrubs grow to about 9 feet with twisted gray trunks and protruding branches ending in sharp spikes.[6]
- Ancient Egyptians burned pellets of myrrh to repel fleas.[6]
- Egyptian Queen Hatshepsut desired to plant myrrh trees all around the temple of the god, Amon. She sent to Africa for the trees. Her successful mission was depicted on the walls of the temple built to enclose her tomb[6]
- First century A.D. Arabia produced about 448 tons of myrrh each year.[7]
- Remnants of the routes through the wilderness used to transport myrrh, frankincense, and other exotic spices may still be seen on satellite images of the area.[8]

Your Turn:

- Produce myrrh and frankincense holiday soap in your kitchen. Search Pinterest or another site for recipes. Which of your friends will enjoy this special gift?
- Find items or containers to decorate representing the wise men's gifts of gold, frankincense, and myrrh. Give it a special place in your holiday decorating.

---

[6] http://www.encyclopedia.com/plants-and-animals/plants/plants/myrrh (accessed 7/1/2017)

[7] http://primaryfacts.com/5511/what-is-myrrh-facts-and-information/ (accessed 7/1/2017)

[8] http://sallysorganics.com/frankincense-2/frankincense-interesting-facts/ (accessed 7/1/2017)

- Following the example of the three gifts brought to Jesus by the wise men, many families have adopted the idea of three gifts for their children at Christmas. We especially like the idea of the "A Wise Man's Christmas Gift Plan" you will find at the link below. [9]
- Make Gold, Frankincense and Myrrh bath bombs. The ones in the link below include real gold mica. [10]
- Diffuse myrrh during your quiet time. Put yourself in Mary's sandals. What thoughts would you be pondering if you were His mom and holding Baby Jesus?

---

[9] http://www.gatherandgrow.co/wise-christmas-gift-plan/ (accessed 7/1/2017)

[10] http://www.humblebeeandme.com/gold-frankin7cense-myrrh-bath-bombs/#more-12794 (accessed 9/23/2017)

Chapter 2

Cedarwood
The Joy of Protection

Cinnamah-Brosia and Friends Share About
Cedarwood – The Joy of Protection

Diffusing Today: Cedarwood and Balsam essential oils
Aromatic Influence: May help provide a sense of calm, relaxation, and grounding
Daily Delight: Cream Cheese Pumpkin Bars
Musically: ***O Little Town of Bethlehem***
Verse of the Day:
> *The righteous person faces many troubles,*
> *but the Lord comes to the rescue each time.*
> ~Psalm 34:19 (NLT)

Joy to the World played in the background as Kaitlyn and her friends gathered at The Coffee Cottage one early December morning. Kaitlyn and Trevor recently announced their engagement. The girls enjoyed their warm beverages and anticipated the fun awaiting them shopping for the perfect bridesmaids' dresses. Kaitlyn's phone rang interrupting their conversation. She allowed the call to filter to her voicemail. Text messages ruled among these young ladies, but the caller persisted. She answered the third call from the number.

The call came from the hospital. Trevor's dad relayed information about an accident. Paramedics had transported Trevor to the local hospital.

Plans changed abruptly. Cinnamah-B hung a sign in The Coffee Cottage window advising of the family emergency. The cottage closed for the day. Everyone accompanied Kaitlyn to the hospital instead. Trevor's dad greeted us, and he and Kaitlyn disappeared to see Trevor and his mom. His expression revealed little. In the waiting room the group prayed together.

Kaitlyn's best friend, Brooke, opened her Bible app and read these words and prayed them over Trevor:

When you go through deep waters, I will be with you. When you go through rivers of difficulty, you will not drown. When you walk through the fire of oppression, you will not be burned up; the flames will not consume you.
~Isaiah 43:23 (NLT)

Have mercy on me, O God, have mercy! I look to you for protection. I will hide beneath the shadow of your wings until the danger passes by.
~Psalm 57:1 (NLT)

And then we waited. The four of them emerged 30 minutes later with smiles on their faces. Trevor wore a bandage on one leg. We laughed at his one jeans leg much shorter than the other. Everyone hugging and speaking at once, his dad finally managed some order among our excited group. "Please let Trevor tell you himself what occurred this morning."

Our eyes and ears tuned in. "When I left for work this morning no matter where I went on the radio dial, Christian music came out," Trevor said. "Country stations, rock stations, jazz stations — or at least I thought — pumped nothing but Christian music into the truck. In my initial efforts to locate something else I missed my turn and found myself in an area of heavy road construction. As I turned down a side street to turn around, the driver of a large piece of heavy equipment turned out in front of me. Initially hidden from each other's view, he came at me fairly quickly. He stopped abruptly, but not before that thing smashed the whole front of my car.

"There is no explanation how I landed in the back seat. All the impact had been to the front. I have a gash on my leg - rather insignificant but earned me this cool new fashion trend." He stared at his mismatched pants legs.

"Here's the deal. I'm sure there was someone in the car with me. The back of my seat must have broken. I felt Him grab my arm and tug me backwards. He sat there with me until the paramedics arrived. Worship songs continued to flow from the destroyed sound system."

His mom's phone rang interrupting Trevor's story. It was his boss, Stan. "Is Trevor okay? I called to check on him since he hasn't arrived at work." After briefly sharing the story, she assured Stan, Trevor received only minor cuts and would heal quickly.

With a sigh of relief echoing through the phone, Stan explained. "I heard about a fiery three-car accident just past that exit about the time Trevor usually travels that way. His uncharacteristic tardiness with no communication convinced me he was involved in it. I know one person died at the scene, and another may have been critically injured."

Stunned by what already transpired along with this added information, Trevor spoke again. "Wow! That's a scary thought, I may have been right in the middle of that incident. Let me finish the story." Trevor took a moment to repeat the first part of the incident to Stan, then continued, "I was concerned about the safety of the other man in the car with me. When I asked the paramedics, they said there was no one else. The way it all came down there is only one person it could have been. I'm certain Jesus or one of His angels was with me through the whole ordeal." The moment became church for them. They joined in a prayer of thanksgiving, and saved their previous plans for another day. Today they celebrated!

Life can change in a moment? Trevor was alive and spared serious injuries. God often allows things to turn out differently, but still for His glory. Think of times when God has provided protection for you or your family in ways unexplainable apart from Him. For those times where God allowed a more challenging outcome how, in hindsight, do you still see His hand in it all? No matter what life looks like, the Christmas carol Joy to the World proclaims the message, 'Great joy is found in the Lord! He is come. He is with us.' Find a favorite version of the familiar carol and play it now. Sing along at the top of your lungs. Let the world know your joy is in Him – no matter the circumstances, and it's available to them, too!

The Essence of Cedarwood in Scripture

Amazing Cedarwood

Botanical Name:
*Cedrus libani; essential oil steam distilled from the bark;
native to: Mountains of Eastern Mediterranean Basin*

Mid-Century Modern style punctuates today's home improvement shows! A well-known furniture company of the era (1950s and 1960s) gifted female high school graduates with miniature cedar chests. Each girl anticipated the larger purchase her family would make – a full size cedar chest that would treasure her hopes for her future marriage and home. The cedar lining of the chest protected handmade quilts and other fine linens and woolens from the ravages of insects, humidity, etc. There was no need for my family to make that purchase. My grandfather, a master carpenter, crafted mine when I was just seven years old.

Free from knots, sturdy in nature, and protected from rot, decay and insects by its thick resin[11], Solomon chose cedarwood to build his palace and the Temple in Jerusalem. He later prayed for wisdom, but God may have answered before he asked considering the great wisdom of building with this material. Even animals find protection and recharging in the wild, resting under its branches at night.

> *"This is what the Sovereign Lord says: I will take a branch from the top of a tall cedar, and I will plant it on the top of Israel's highest mountain. It will become a majestic cedar, sending forth its branches and producing seed. Birds of every sort will nest in it, finding shelter in the shade of its branches.*
> ~Ezekiel 17:22-23 (NLT)

---

[11] http://www.streetdirectory.com/travel_guide/32566/home_improvement/cedar_wood_benefits.html (accessed 9/23/2017)

> *which was once like a cedar of Lebanon, with beautiful branches that cast deep forest shade . . . The birds nested in its branches and in its shade all the wild animals gave birth*
>
> ~Ezekiel 31:3b, 6a (NLT)

Cedarwood dominated the construction industry in Solomon's day and well beyond. Wonder if their endeavors resulted in cedar trees on the endangered list during this time? Moving forward, consider what materials first century A.D. construction workers incorporated in the building of barns and stables. Remember as son to King David, Solomon and his family came from Bethlehem. Was the cedarwood tradition as common there as in Jerusalem? Was Jesus born in a cedar stable? The stable protected the innkeeper's livestock, and on the night of His birth it protected the most important treasure of our eternal future?

God's ultimate gift of His Son born to bring us salvation provides the best protection ever, everywhere, and all the time. Preceding His birth by many centuries, a psalmist proclaimed:

> *The righteous thrive like a palm tree and grow like a cedar tree in Lebanon. Planted in the house of the LORD, they thrive in the courts of our God. They will still bear fruit in old age, healthy and green, to declare: "The LORD is just; He is my rock and there is no unrighteousness in Him."*
>
> ~Psalm 92:12-15

Perhaps because of their nature, God had the psalmist compare the righteous to cedar trees. The trees often attain the age of 2,000 years. They invite life (birds and animals) under the protection of their limbs. Those who trust and follow Jesus thrive to proclaim His birth – and death and resurrection – inviting others into the protective covering of Jesus!

In the New Testament, the apostle, Paul, tells us our bodies are the temple where the Holy Spirit's presence now resides. Link that with the Old Testament analogy of the righteous growing like cedar trees. So Jesus lives within us. Our faith grows. He is our protection. We flourish like a cedar tree. Now that blows my mind! How about yours? Trust the Baby Boy born in a stable. He offers us divine protection. We experience growth produced by the Holy Spirit in our lives.

> *Don't you know that your body is a sanctuary of the Holy Spirit who is in you, whom you have from God? You are not your own, for you were bought at a price. Therefore glorify God in your body.*
>
> ~1 Corinthians 6:19-20

Cedar is common Christmas decorating material. Candles laced with cedar's aroma are a favorite during the holiday season. Christmas wreaths grace our doors, often created with cedar or pine branches. It is unlikely the tradition of the cedar was originally tied to these Bible verses or even to the thought the stable may have been cedar. But we can look back and see meaningfulness for the season in every cedar bough and wreath and every cedar scented candle.

Wreaths are often crafted from cedar boughs and other evergreens. Since we are speaking of cedar, let's take a side-trip into the meaning of the wreath. No definitive history of the evergreen circle exists, but some believe the wreath was first used as a symbol of victory in Ancient Rome. Ties to both Christian and pagan origin are found. From a Christian point of view, the circle symbolizes eternity with Jesus. The branches are evergreen - review Psalm 92:12-15 above for that one. Added holly signified the crown of thorns, its berries - the drops of blood Jesus would shed for us. Jesus protects us. His death assures us of His protection of our eternal life. In victory He will come again to take us to heaven.

Today's wreaths feature every color of creation, every material under God's big yellow sun, and are decorated with a vast assortment of trinkets and treasures. I am well aware many of these wreaths glorify areas of our lives other than Jesus. Will you get really creative with me? Meditate on stories of protection and renewal in your life and in your walk with Him. His protection is victory. The wreath may serve as a joyful reminder – like victory a wreath. Create a wreath that glorifies God's hand in your life. What will you include on your wreath and why?

A Woman of the Bible's Experience the Joy of Protection
Rahab's Divine Escape

"Even in terrible circumstances and calamities, in matters of life and death, if I sense that I am in the shadow of God, I find light, so much light that my vision improves dramatically. I know that holiness is near."[12]
~Kathleen Norris

We crept up the winding mountain sheet of slippery glass. Ice-covered, it hardly resembled a road. The storm moved in quickly, and the mountain loomed between our current location and home. As long as all the cars kept moving along slowly, progress continued. Then several cars ahead, one person chose to stop. My husband skillfully maneuvered our vehicle every cautious way he knew in an attempt to a stop short of the long snaking line of cars ahead of us. Less than a foot to go and we had not slowed one itty-bitty bit. At the last possible instant we felt a gentle rush of wings filled with a giant pillow swoop down and under us, lifting our car and setting it down ever so softly less than an inch from a guaranteed collision. We arrived home safely. I retain no recollection of the remainder of the trip. In our joy-filled awe of the moment, we gave pause to praise God for protection with no explanation aside from Him. I'm reminded of an Old Testament story of divine protection.

God directed the Israelites to enter and take the Promised Land. Trumpets blared as Israelites circled, and the walls came crashing down. One tiny section of the Jericho wall remained standing. Apart from God's divine intervention, no reason exists for Rahab's home, alone, to be spared.

Rehab, a prostitute, knew stories of God's protection for the Israelites. Forty years earlier God miraculously delivered them on

---

[12] Kathleen Norris, *Amazing Grace: A Vocabulary of Faith*, (New York, New York: Riverhead Books, 1998) page 31.

dry ground between water walls of the parted Red Sea. The same sea walls collapsed, gobbling up the Egyptians on their heels. Memory of the event remained fresh in the minds of residents in surrounding countries. Perhaps they gained more than an ounce of healthy respect for Israel's God, too. Rehab did, and His ways spared her and her family from certain death.

God instructed Joshua to lead the charge to enter the Promised Land, wiping out heathen nations as they went. Rahab offered information and protection to the Israelite spies.. You know she shook from the inside out, causing her knees to knock like castanets and setting her heart to racing as she contemplated the possibilities. What if everything went wrong? Aware of the risks, she chose to help the spies.

In return the spies instructed Rahab to gather her family, tie a red cord to her window, and wait out the coming destruction. They would return for every one of them if she followed their orders. True to their word, her little corner never succumbed. The men rescued Rahab and her family.

Imagine her telling the story to her son, Boaz. Boaz shared with his son, Obed, Obed with Jesse, and Jesse with David, who became Israel's first king. That's right! King David's family tree includes Rahab, his great-great grandmother, honored to be included in the Nativity story via the genealogy of Jesus.

Salmon fathered Boaz by Rahab, Boaz fathered Obed by Ruth, Obed fathered Jesse,
~Matthew 1:5

Stories of Rahab's red cord and our angel with the pillow proclaim God's amazing protection. Ours did not require a politically unfavorable decision as Rahab's did. But like cedars growing strong through personal experiences with God, we proclaim:

"He is our rock! There is no unrighteousness in Him."
~Psalm 92:15

Read Rahab's story in the Bible in the book of Joshua, chapters 1, 2, and 6. What is your story of unusual protection/provision that could only be orchestrated by God? Share the joy you found in that moment.

Cedarwood Essence Droplets

But let all who take refuge in You rejoice; let them shout for joy forever. May You shelter them, and may those who love Your name boast about You.
~Psalm 5:11

Fun Facts:

- Legend has it ships for Alexander the Great were to be constructed of cedars from Lebanon.
- Cedarwood hardwood is a natural insect repellent often used in closets and chests to protect the contents.
- Cedarwood was a common material for the construction of Native American canoes.[13]
- Western Red Cedar is often used for guitar soundboards and Spanish Cedar for the necks of the guitars.[13]
- Cedar trees grow up to 200 feet tall.[15]
- The cones on a male cedar tree are egg-shaped; on a female tree they are barrel-shaped.[14]
- In some regions, cedar trees are commonly used as Christmas trees.

Your Turn:
- At bedtime combine lavender and cedarwood oils. Diffuse to create a restful atmosphere.
- Cedarwood is a common material for woodworking projects large and small. Do a quick internet or Pinterest

---

[13] http://www.softschools.com/facts/plants/cedar_facts/1280/ (accessed 6/21/2017)
[14] https://www.pineconesplus.com/blog/2014/03/fun-facts-about-cedar-a-craft-project-for-easter/ (accessed 6/21/2017)
[15] https://www.reference.com/home-garden/interesting-cedar-trees-9784bb3753d68673 (accessed 6/21/2017)

search for some fabulous ideas. Share your creation with us on our Facebook page.[16]
- Quick growing cedar trees are easy to cultivate. Plant one in your yard. Enjoy the fragrance, too.[17]
- Cedar chests protect valuable contents from insect damage, and traditionally store hopes for tomorrow. When the lid is opened we're greeted with aromas that may transport us into moments of wisdom learned from life's memories. Find or build a miniature cedar chest. Fill it with Scriptures and memories that give you hope for the future. Open and reminisce in times of trouble, recalling the God moments of protection and provision. Potential is great for this becoming a treasured family heirloom.

---

[16] http://www.facebook.com/lynnuwatsonwriter (accessed 6/21/2017)
[17] https://www.gardeningknowhow.com/ornamental/trees/cedar/growing-cedar-trees.htm (accessed 6/21/2017)

Chapter 3

Frankincense

The Joy of Forgiveness

Cinnamah-Brosia and Friends Share about
Frankincense – The Joy of Forgiveness

Diffusing Today: Frankincense & Myrrh
Aromatic Influence: May help create a spiritually uplifting environment
Daily Delight: Chocolate Covered Animal Cookies
Musically: ***The Lord's Prayer*** (Andrea Bocelli)
Verse of the day:
> *Soak me in your laundry and I'll come out clean,*
> *scrub me and I'll have a snow-white life.*
> *Tune me in to foot-tapping songs,*
> *set these once-broken bones to dancing.*
> *~Psalm 51:7-8 (The Message)*

~~Let these words from Cinnamah Brosia from a blogpost dated May 14, 2017 introduce the story:

When your birthday is May 14, some years it inevitably falls on Mother's Day. Like me, you may love the day because your own children are sure to remember and shower you with unending love. Maybe also like me, you hate the day because memories surface of the mother often absent and negligent in your life. This was one of those years for me.

I revealed much of my childhood story in ***The Essence of Courage***. I never understood why my mother felt compelled to hurt Gram and Gramps, my siblings, and me. This year, a day before my birthday, a card arrived along with a note. I'm certain she never sent me one before. My thinking gears, laced with more than a bit of anxiety and paranoia, whizzed and whirred out of control. I collapsed into a comfy chair in Sophia's corner. Overcome with nausea and anticipating poison words, I reluctantly began to read:

Dear Cinnamon,

There's no easy way to say this, except I have wronged you and all of my family so much. A do-over remains out of reach, but I would like to start fresh.

When your Gram died, wheelbarrows of regret heaped themselves all over me. If I wasn't ashamed of my actions before, I am now. Over a year now since her passing, I'm begging you to allow me to share my side of the story. Please meet me at the Coffee Cottage at 3 PM on your birthday.

I dare not sign this Mom — So for now,
Simply,
Sandra

* * * * * * * * *

She found me on Facebook. She, of course, knew where to send the card. I found her on my birthday standing at the door of The Coffee Cottage, her appearance much more weathered than I imagined. A gleam sparkled in her eyes in spite of it — one I never witnessed as a child.

What prompted me to say "yes" to this moment? I believed I had forgiven her long ago, but the thought of reconciliation required a level of grace I didn't know whether or not I could provide. Was it even safe to entertain such a thought? Memories of my mother's hideous parenting failures clawed my heart raw. Gram taught forgiveness for every wrong, and her lessons played ping-pong in every corner of my mind. My whole life I've sought an explanation for why my mother and her friends inflicted abuse.

Her note expressed regrets. She claimed her life is changed, and she desires to mend our brokenness. A do-over impossible, she questioned if I would at least allow us a fresh start. I puzzled over why I would, but there we stood, face to face. Her face bent down and with a hand posed on her chest, she shuffled her feet

My apprehension punctuated by curiosity, I invited her in. Several uncomfortable moments later Sandra Porter and I made our way to Sophia's Corner, a spot familiar to her before I arrived in this world. As her eyes darted about the space, taking in the changes, I prayed for more wisdom than this corner had ever witnessed before, and for a strong clamp on a tongue ready to lash out for every wound recalled.

Her focus lingered on the wall behind me. During the renovation Kaitlyn discovered an old animal cracker tin containing a button-covered piece of blue jeans. She repurposed the piece into artwork for The Coffee Cottage. Fascinated by her imaginings of stories that may be stitched in, Kaitlyn eagerly added the piece of history to our new look. We never imagined the pains from my mother's childhood buttoned into the denim.

"Learning of your grandmother's death last year unleashed excruciating pain in my spirit. Probably no surprise to you, I drowned it in pain killers and alcohol. In a hospital bed seven weeks later, awakening from that particular nightmare, I struggled to focus on the gentlest eyes and kindest smile ever. It was Andy – your father. His expression spoke tenderness I didn't believe I had ever witnessed before. I recalled moments over the last couple years when maybe he had shown more kindness, but always under the influence of drugs and alcohol, I just didn't get it.

"I continued flitting in and out of his life like I had yours. That never changed. He begged me to visit Mom with him two years ago. I convinced myself I had no interest. Forgiveness for how badly she and your gramps hurt me never winked in one tiny corner of my heart. So, there I was in the hospital room, connected to a bunch of machines and tubes. I was unable to kick him out.

"Oh, Andy relished the opportunity to share how he reconnected with all of you a few years ago and how his heart had softened to this Jesus your Gram always crammed down my throat. He announced, 'I'm a Jesus-follower.' Weird, but his face radiated a change. I attempted to tune him out anyway. Obvious to me now, God had special plans for my confinement. One of Mom's often quoted Bible verses popped in my head. I hadn't thought about any of them in years, and now I questioned, 'Is there really hope for a new start for even me.'"

For I know the plans I have for you, says the Lord, plans for welfare and not for evil, to give you a future and a hope.
~Jeremiah 29:11 (RSV)

Not sure how to address this woman — Sandra? Mother? Mom? — I simply shared my perspective. "After the abuse Blossom, Stone, and I suffered at his hands and yours, fear and skepticism surrounded those first meetings with Dad. I wondered if his new relationship with Jesus was a cover for yet another chance to manipulate for selfish purposes. Forgiveness came slowly — one tiny bit at a time."

Tears rolled down Sandra's wrinkled cheeks as she jumped back to her story. "Cinnamon, you didn't know your grandfather when it happened. His brother John died in a boating accident. The two of them and their buds fished and drank the river dry – so to speak. Their macho egos kicked in. They attempted some goofy shenanigans in the boat. Uncle John drowned when he fell overboard. His head had crashed into the bow. In a sick sort of way because of Uncle John's unnatural affections toward me, his death made me happy.

"I shared it all with Andy – not another soul. First I told him about the buttons. Seeing them on the wall earlier was another reminder. I had been pricked by the needle so many times, sewing button after button on to the leg of those old jeans. Every time I felt wronged as a child, Mom reminded me how many times Jesus tells us to forgive. Unless she observed forgiveness in my heart, she required me to add a button to that hunk of blue jean fabric — at least one for each offense. I rarely forgave, so there were 'millions' of buttons. Those buttons on the wall represent a small sampling of pain from my childhood.

"It was pointless to confide in Mom about Uncle John. Deep down I believed she knew, but closed her eyes and mind to the damage he inflicted. How many buttons would be required for this if I brought it up? And if she judged it a lie – well, I couldn't even think about that? Contemplating how many more buttons would be required, I chose not to go there. Not happening. Not happening again. Did Mom know about Uncle John's disgusting behavior? Did she care? Did Dad care? I didn't care!

"The accident changed everything. Dad worked out of necessity, came home, and settled into the porch swing, making it his perch. Sober then, he fixed his blank stare on who knows what. After two long years he announced he met Jesus out there in the garden. He radiated joy – EVERYWHERE! And his life needed holy purpose now. Really?

"His purpose: sharing Jesus with every one of my friends who walked in the door. Nauseating! His interest in them was way more than any he had shown in my life."

During Sandra's brief pause I said, "I bet that hurt. You felt embarrassed too, didn't you? And at the same time, you were probably jealous of the attention he gave them. I would have been."

Sandra said, "Yes, yes, and yes. Andy worked hard at the grocery store, and living a hippie life style pulled us in. What fun to make a baby and live in a van covered in flowers and peace signs! Our so-called friends' moral values mocked everything mom held dear. She cried for weeks while begging us to follow Jesus instead of the world of drugs, sex, and rock-n-roll. Oh, if she only knew!"

My turn to speak again, and my heart filled with questions. Oh, how could she believe such lies! Sandra assessed the situation from a much different vantage point than me, at a time before I was born. I responded respectfully. "Gram did know. Gramps confessed everything. You perceived it all as rejection. Gramps loved you so much he allowed you to follow your own path. His own failures as a parent and watching you self-destruct, convinced him of your unwillingness to forgive. Instead, he chose to pour everything into your friends. His love for Jesus and the thought of even one more young person following a wayward path without his effort to be Jesus to them, percolated within him. He faithfully prayed you would see the Truth. He loved you that much!"

Her lips began to quiver as a tear drop rolled down her cheek. The only words she mustered, "You knew?"

"Sandra — Dad brought all the questions to Gram when he came back. She patiently answered, filling in all the missing pieces of your story." Clearing my throat, my eyebrows rising to the sky and heart beating a little faster, I said, "We all prayed for the day Jesus would change your life, too. Your note came as a potential and long-awaited answer to many prayers, but I remained skeptical. My past niggles at me to discount your words, and continue to exclude you from my life. Gram would have me sewing an awful lot of buttons, wouldn't she?

"You remember, Gram did have a Scripture for everything. I loved that about her. I hear her proclaiming these words from Jesus:

> *'For if you forgive men their trespasses, your heavenly Father also will forgive you; but if you do not forgive men their trespasses, neither will your Father forgive your trespasses.'*
> ~John 6:14-15 (RSV)"

A tiny voice whispered in my ear to call her mom.

"Mom, let's start over."

Cascading like a waterfall down our cheeks, tears stabbed our eyes. We squeezed out years of damage in an embrace promising to last a lifetime.

"Cinnamon, Psalm 32 speaks of the joy of forgiveness. I've super-glued the words to my heart." With the ravages of years of despair washed over by the joy of Jesus now etched on her face, Mom pleaded, "Cinnamon, read it with me, please."

> *How joyful is the one whose transgression is forgiven, whose sin is covered! How joyful is the man the Lord does not charge with sin and in whose spirit is no deceit! …Many pains come to the wicked, but the one who trusts in the Lord will have faithful love surrounding him. Be glad in the Lord and rejoice, you righteous ones; shout for joy, all you upright in heart.*
> ~Psalm 32:1-2; 10-11

Read the entire Psalm in a Bible version of your choice. Make it your prayer to live a life of forgiving and being forgiven. Great joy is found there!

The Essence of Frankincense in Scripture
Will We Smell Him Coming?

Botanic Name: Boswellia carterii; oil is steam-distilled from the resin "tears," where cuts were made in the bark of the tree; native to Southwest Arabian peninsula, Ethiopia and Somalia

The popular White Elephant holiday party game (sometimes called Dirty Santa) often requires forgiveness between players. Is that an understatement? For those unfamiliar with the game, everyone has a number. Everyone brings a wrapped item and adds it to the gift pile. Going in turn (by number) each player chooses a gift from the pile, or 'steals' one from another player. The gifts are open as they are chosen. If it's something really good, the player who has it will do their best to hide it or distract another player who may wish to steal it. The game can become a friendly – or maybe not so friendly – battle. Depending on the contestants the coveted 'gift' may be a movie or coffee shop gift card, a beautiful fashion accessory, or dinner at a fav restaurant. At one party my husband and I attended, the item fought over — are you ready — a case of bathroom tissue! That is pretty valuable, I must admit, and much forgiveness was required as the 'white elephant' was stolen time and again.

White elephants remind me of the elephants and myriad circus animals parading around the old animal cracker tin we discovered in Cinnamah-Brosia's last story. Gram stored the forgiveness buttons in the tin. What prompted her choice of storage containers? Was the tin just lying around begging for a new purpose, or did she love the circus?

A friend spent one year traveling with a well-known circus troupe. She occasionally rode an elephant as they paraded around the arena for the big show. She observed animals whose trainers treated them like family, fiercely protective. In a recent conversation, she and I lamented the loss of the circus. I am aware that opinions vary on the subject, but the conversation piqued my interest to learn if elephants are forgiving animals.

Truth is, they are! In the wild this mammoth creature suffers many injustices at the hands of man and his greed, their lives sacrificed for his pleasure. Rather than vengeance, over and over again elephants display trust in spite of their physical and emotional wounds. They form amazing bonds with those who help them, but also return and forgive those who have harmed them and/or their elephant family.[19]

Forgiveness came through animal sacrifice in the Old Testament. In the New Testament, Jesus came as the Ultimate Sacrifice. Old Testament sacrifices required pure unblemished lambs. He sacrificed His life as *the* pure and unblemished Lamb of God. Triumphant over the grave, He reigns supreme as the Lion of Judah, the King of all Kings. He further serves in the role of our High Priest.

All through history anointing oil set apart priests and kings for their duties. Frankincense earned its reputation as the aroma of kings. The kings' caravan of Nativity fame, carried the aroma of frankincense (and myrrh) on their arduous journey from the East. Their gift to the Christ child acknowledged His kingship. Ancient records leading them to the infant, Jesus, convinced them He was the Promised King of Kings.

> *After Jesus was born in Bethlehem of Judea in the days of King Herod, wise men from the east arrived unexpectedly in Jerusalem, saying, "Where is He who has been born King of the Jews? For we saw His star in the east and have come to worship Him."*
>
> ~Matthew 2:1-2

---

[19] https://wildlifeproject.wordpress.com/2013/07/12/unbelievably-elephants-forgive/ (accessed 9/15/2017)

The ancient texts reveal frankincense' importance in the sacrificial rituals from the time God first introduced them to Moses.

> *The Lord said to Moses: "Take fragrant spices: stacte, onycha, and galbanum; the spices and pure frankincense are to be in equal measures. Prepare expertly blended incense from these; it is to be seasoned with salt, pure and holy.*
>
> ~Exodus 30:34-35

Moses family hailed from the tribe of Levi. God chose Moses' brother Aaron, Aaron's sons and descendants to burn the incense (which when mentioned in the Bible, always includes frankincense) in their high priestly roles. Frankincense' aroma filled the temple and arose to the throne of God each day as incense was burned on the altar where God met with His people. Once a year the high priest entered the holy of holies, cleansing the horns of the altar with the blood of the sin offering.

> *Place this altar just outside of the veil that conceals the covenant chest and the seat of mercy that sits on top of the covenant chest. I will meet with you there.*
> *Aaron is to burn fragrant incense on it every morning when he trims the lamps' wicks and every evening when he lights the lamps. Incense must be burned in My presence throughout all your generations. Do not burn any strange incense, burnt offerings, or grain offerings at this altar. Also, do not pour out any drink offerings on it. Since this altar is sacred to Me, Aaron is to cleanse it once each year by smearing blood from the sin offering on its horns. Throughout all your generations, the high priests are to perform this ritual.*
>
> ~Exodus 30:6-10 (VOICE)

Our granddaughter loves to ever so quietly sneak up on the unsuspecting person as she enters a room. She hopes they will squeal confirming they never heard her coming. The high priests saturated in the aromas of the sacrifice (which included frankincense) had no pleasure in surprising anyone. Everywhere they went the aroma preceded them. Revelation proclaims the prayers of the saints continue to ascend to the Lamb. Jesus' robes and hair and person are saturated in the aromas. On the great and glorious day He comes for His people, will we catch the aroma of His heavenly caravan almost before we see Him, as if that were possible?

> *When He took the scroll, the four living creatures and the 24 elders fell down before the Lamb. Each one had a harp and gold bowls filled with incense, which are the prayers of the saints.*
>
> ~Revelation 5:8

God's initial instructions for forgiveness required an annual ritual throughout all generations. Throughout the Old Testament, aromas ascended to God's throne in heaven from the Temple Holy of Holies — the very place set aside for God's love and mercy. Priests performed the ritual of burning the incense (chosen by lot) only once in their lifetime, if at all. As the New Testament opens Zachariah was the chosen priest to perform the duty. He meets an angel in that holy place. Speechlessness caught him as he exited, but we can be sure the aroma was powerful. He stood in the presence of the Holy God. He learned from the angel, although doubting the truth of it, he and his wife, Elizabeth, would have a baby in their old age. The baby, John the Baptist, preceded Jesus in his ministry, preparing the people to receive their Messiah. Read Zachariah's story in Luke 1.

A Woman of the Bible Experiences the Joy of Forgiveness

Jesus Told Her Everything She Ever Did

Forgiveness is the giving, and so the receiving, of life.[19]
~George MacDonald

    She lived a complicated life. She had had five husbands. She had been divorced five times. Now she lived with a man refusing to give her his name. Did she have children? Maybe she had a few and was a step-mom to others. Talk about a blended family! She came to the well alone in the midday's heat. Other women called her names - and not pretty ones either. They judged her life without removing the log from their own eyes. Women often have a tribe of close friends. They do life together. What lonely agony resided in that place for her?

    My heart still aches fifty-plus years later recalling the pain of "slam books" in junior high. My family moved so often. Seventh grade, another new school, the new girl didn't fit in — a recipe for disaster. We live in an age now where almost everything goes by an acronym. It's rare anyone remembers what the letters even stand for. Classmates had them in the seventh grade for their slam books. Big difference though - no one ever forgot what the letter codes stood for. The ones used to describe me were never kind. We moved away before eighth grade. I no longer had to face these bullies, but to this day I clearly remember one of those acronyms boldly placed on my page in their books. The woman at the well permanently resided in her neighborhood. She faced the bullies everyday for years.

    She encounters a man asking for a drink of water. She recognizes the unseemliness of his request. After all racial tension existed between her Samaritan heritage and this man's Jewishness.

---

[19]https://www.brainyquote.com/authors/george_macdonald (accessed 10/2/2017)

The conversation focuses on this well — an heirloom Jacob first provided to his son Joseph. Jesus carried no cup or bucket to drink the water He requested, which prompted the conversation. In a holy switch-up, Jesus offered Living Water to this marginalized woman. Her curiosity aroused, Jesus instructed her to go home, return with her husband, and He would tell her the rest of the story. No doubt His opinion of her would sink straight to the bottom of the well, but she responded honestly.

> *"I don't have a husband," she answered.*
> *"You have correctly said, 'I don't have a husband,'" Jesus said. "For you've had five husbands, and the man you now have is not your husband. What you have said is true."*
> ~John 4:17-18

Wow! She stayed, and He told her everything she had ever done. He offered His forgiveness and revealed His identity. She recognized, believed, embraced, and worshipped Him. Returning to town she shared the Gospel with all the men. You heard that correctly. She ran right back to the men, but this time with the Good News! This nameless woman presented a very different exuberance and joy than before. First century men placed little value on anything a woman had to say, but she told *all* the men. Instead of ignoring her, they chose to leave what they were doing and go find Jesus. What thoughts occupied the minds of the women bullies now? I pray they found forgiveness for her in their hearts, too.

> *If we claim that we're free of sin, we're only fooling ourselves. A claim like that is errant nonsense. On the other hand, if we admit our sins—make a clean breast of them—he won't let us down; he'll be true to himself. He'll forgive our sins and purge us of all wrongdoing. If we claim that we've never sinned, we out-and-out contradict God—make a liar out of him. A claim like that only shows off our ignorance of God.*
> ~1 John 1:8-10 (The Message)

We all require God's forgiveness. Whatever your shortcomings, tell them to God. He knows them already. Ask for and accept His forgiveness. Forgive yourself. Forgive others, too. Send frankincense' aroma heavenward to the throne of Jesus, our sacrificial Lamb.

Frankincense Essence Droplets

The young women will dance for joy, and the men—old and young—will join in the celebration. I will turn their mourning into joy. I will comfort them and exchange their sorrow for rejoicing.
~Jeremiah 31:13 (NLT)

Fun Facts:
- Frankincense is sometimes referred to as liquid gold.[20]
- Frankincense is native to southern Arabia. Due to high demand for the substance in the ancient world, the area bore the title "Arabia the Blessed."[21]
- The ancient writer, Herodotus, wrote the Arabian frankincense trees were protected by dragons of all sizes, and the rumor spread.[19]
- In ancient cultures the purest clearest frankincense resin was chewed like gum.[19]
- From archeology and from ancient texts proof exists frankincense was used medicinally, being a staple of Chinese medicine since 500 B.C.[22]
- When the Roman Empire toppled and Christianity was on the rise, the use of incense was forbidden due to its frequent associations with pagan worship. It remains among the gifts presented to Jesus. The Roman Catholic Church was first to bring it back into Christian worship.[20]

Your Turn:
- Create a personal altar for your quiet time. Diffuse frankincense to help create a more meditative aura around you. You'll find several diffusers that have a spiritual look to them. Remembering that frankincense goes up to Jesus

---

[20] http://www.hollandandbarrett.com/advice-articles/seasonal-wellbeing/5-facts-frankincense/ (accessed 6/26/2017
[21] https://www.annmariegianni.com/7-things-you-didnt-know-about-frankincense-essential-oil/ (accessed 6/26/2017)
[22] http://www.history.com/news/a-wise-mans-cure-frankincense-and-myrrh (accessed 6/26/2017)

with the prayers of the saints, the same aroma surrounds you.
- Gifts of the Magi: Gold, Frankincense, and Myrrh is a wonderful little book with historic artwork, stories of the magi and includes small replicas of gold, silver, and myrrh. This is a keepsake in our Christmas celebration, the tiny replicas of the gifts be placed with the baby in our nativity set.[25]
- Purchase or make your own frankincense soap. (Many recipes for it are available online in written and video format.) When you use it allow it to be a reminder of God's powerful acts of forgiveness, allowing His only Son, Jesus, to die in our place.

---

[25] Carolyn Vaughan, *The Gifts of the MAGI* (New York, New York: The Metropolitan Museum of Art and Bullfinch Press/Little Brown and Company, 1998).

Chapter 4

Rose
The Joy of Love

Cinnamon Brosia and Friends Share About
Rose – The Joy of Love

Diffusing Today: Rose, Orange, and Jasmine essential oils
Aromatic Influence: Invites warmth, togetherness, and spiritual well-being
Special of the Day: Decorated cut out sugar cookies
Musically: **Love Came Down** (Kari Jobe)
Verse of the Day:
> *The earth is full of the Lord's unfailing love.*
> ~Psalm 33:5b

Cookie dough, icing, food color, sprinkles, and cookie cutters all assembled. Excitement reigned for Lily today, her imagination actively dreaming of the Christmas cookie possibilities. Seven-year-old Lily, honorary director of operations for the sugar-cookie-decorating extravaganza assured me all was ready. With at least fifteen minutes until the other children brought their moms for the party, we hopped over to Sophia's Corner, getting comfy in the overstuffed turquoise chairs by the fireplace.

"Ms. Cinna-Bro, my friend, Molly, has a new baby sister. Her name is Olivia. Her mom said they adopted her. What does adopt mean?"

"Lily, you ask a great question. The family choosing to adopt invites the child to be a part of their family forever. Molly's mommy and daddy are Olivia's mommy and daddy now, too.

That was not the end of Lily's questions, of course! "That's really good for Olivia, right? But why did her mommy not want her?"

"The mommy who had Molly's new sister believed she would not be able to take care of Olivia the way a mommy should. Molly's mom and dad made her a part of their family. She and Molly will always be sisters."

"But why did she believe that? Mommies always take care of their babies. I take care of my baby dolls, too."

"Lily, Mr. Jeremy and I adopted Aaron. His mommy asked us to, because she loved him so much. Sometimes girls have babies when they are not old enough to care for the baby as well as they would like. Mr. Jeremy's cousin, broken-hearted to give her baby away, still believed that was best. We gave Aaron a home and family. We are his mommy and daddy forever. His last name is Fields now, just like ours. Kaitlyn and Caryn are his sisters, too, forever."

"Cinna-Bro, is that why her mommy gave Olivia away? I could never give my dolls away. Will they see each other again?"

"Lily, Olivia's first mommy is sixteen years old. You think she's old, right?" Lily nodded in agreement. "Sixteen is still very young, and she chose to have someone love Olivia and give her a good home."

Lily continued the questioning until others arrived. When Lily's mom, Mandy, arrived with Amber (Molly's mom), Molly and baby Olivia were with them, of course. Molly begged her mom to tell Lily all about Olivia's adoption.

Amber suggested they wait for all the guests to arrive. Everyone gathered around Olivia, patting her, allowing her to grab their fingers, and talking baby talk to her. Lots of giggles and love nearly smothered the little one.

With everyone present, Amber explained to Lily and all Molly's friends how Olivia came to live with them.

"Olivia's mom is sixteen. She lives in a neighborhood with troubles everywhere. She feared for Olivia, because she couldn't always be there for her. She wished Olivia would have opportunities to experience things she couldn't provide. And she chose to finish school."

"So, she just gave her baby away?" It was Lily again.

"That must have been the hardest thing she ever did, Lily," Amber replied. "Mommies love their babies so much. They want the best for them. Sometimes they know they are unable to provide a good home. They allow another family to adopt their baby."

C-B said, "Olivia's mommy knows Molly will be a great big sister, and Molly's parents will love and care for Olivia in ways she cannot. It takes a lot of love to do that. It takes a lot of love from Molly's mom and dad, too, to love Olivia like their own. Molly's mom and dad are Olivia's new mommy and daddy."

"Before we begin decorating cookies, let's read two Bible passages about how much God loves us and adopted us into His family," C-B suggested. "It is a little like Olivia's and Aaron's stories, but even better!"

> *But although he made the world, the world didn't recognize him when he came. Even in his own land and among his own people, the Jews, he was not accepted. Only a few would welcome and receive him. But to all who received him, he gave the right to become children of God. All they needed to do was to trust him to save them. All those who believe this are reborn! — not a physical rebirth resulting from human passion or plan—but from the will of God. And Christ became a human being and lived here on earth among us and was full of loving forgiveness and truth. And some of us have seen his glory—the glory of the only Son of the heavenly Father!*
>
> *~John 1:10-14 (TLB)*

> *But when the right time came, the time God decided on, he sent his Son, born of a woman, born as a Jew, to buy freedom for us who were slaves to the law so that he could adopt us as his very own sons. And because we are his sons, God has sent the Spirit of his Son into our hearts, so now we can rightly speak of God as our dear Father. Now we are no longer slaves but God's own sons. And since we are his sons, everything he has belongs to us, for that is the way God planned.*
>
> *~Galatians 4:4-7 (TLB)*

Molly had something to add. "Dad gave me, Olivia, and Mom each a pink and a red rose the day Olivia came to live at our home. Dad said it was because God loves us so much He adopts us as His children, too. He is our Father, and Jesus is our brother forever. When we believe in Him and trust Him we share heaven — that's His home — with Him forever, too."

"Molly, Know what? Jesus has been called the Christmas Rose," C-B responded.

"Lily questioned, "Jesus is a flower? Cinna-Bro, that's silly!"

"It may seem silly, but colors of roses have meanings too. When we think of Christmas roses we think of red ones. Red roses mean love. Pink roses mean joy. Molly, Olivia, and their mommy and daddy are filled with love and joy for this happening in their family. I believe he gave them the roses to remind them to have Jesus' kind of love and joy all the time, and to show how happy he was that their family includes Oliva now." Cinnamah-Brosia was sure she satisfied Lily's curiosity this time.

Lily persisted. "But Olivia is just a baby. She doesn't know about roses."

And C-B offered this thought. "I believe they will press those roses in a book. They will take pictures of them. They will remind Olivia of the special day she became part of their family. How could we make our cookies special reminders of Jesus' love?"

An idea popped in C-B's mind. "Lily, do we have some raspberry jam in the cupboard?"

"Yes, I saw it. What are we going to do?"

"If we cut out Christmas tree cookies, we spread the jam on one of them, poke holes in the second one and set it on top of the first one, then the red jam will show through like the tree is decorated in Christmas roses. What do you think?"

All the girls jumped and shouted full of excitement — all talking at once.

They busied themselves making the cookies. Another mom recounted to the girls how she was adopted. "My first mommy's decision probably saved me from a lot of difficulties and trouble. I'm thankful that God directed her and my mommy and daddy who adopted me to make the decisions they did."

Amber presented an idea to the girls. "Cinnamah's son, Aaron, is a fireman. He and the other fireman work really hard to protect us. What do you think? We could take some of the cookies to the fire station to thank them. You can even tell them about the roses on the cookies and why we made them that way."

They all agreed. After a quick cleanup the group was on its way to spread the love and joy of Jesus around their community.

Most places do not accept homemade baked goods. If you have access to a commercial kitchen, this may make them acceptable at more locations. We suggested a fire station in the story. They might accept home baked. Be sure you check with the fire station, nursing homes, children's hospitals, etc. to learn their requirements for gift items, baked or otherwise, you take to them.

Another suggestion for sharing the love of the Rose of Bethlehem is offering your time to children and their families confined to the hospital for the holidays. A residential facility for one of our local children's hospitals encourages young people (check age requirements) to come and share dance, arts, puppets and other talents for entertaining and/or teaching the patients. You may be able to take a group to a children's home or hospital residential facility that will allow you to bake cookies with their children in the facility's kitchen. Allow your imagination to soar, check out the rules where you would like to go, and then spread the joyful love of Jesus, too!

NOTE: We found the recipe for making the rose-decorated Christmas tree cookies the girls created in the story. Check it out at this link: http://www.queenofmykitchen.com/raspberry-filled-christmas-tree-cookies/ (accessed 9/15/2017)

The Essence of Rose in Scripture

Jesus, Our Christmas Rose

Botanical Name: Rosa damascena (damsak rose); fragrant oil steam distilled from the petals; native to Turkey, Syria, and Lebanon

"We're singing some weird song in the Christmas program this year," I remember telling my dad after the first rehearsal way back in the fifth grade. Inspired by the Messianic prophecy of Isaiah 11:1, In 1894 Theodore Baker penned the words to the song Lo, How a Rose E'er Blooming. By the 1960s it earned its place among classic Christmas carols, but remained, until then, unknown to me — little ole me at the ripe old age of ten!

> *Then a shoot will grow from the stump of Jesse, and a branch from his roots will bear fruit.*
> ~Isaiah 11:1

Do you see a rose here? Neither do I. An interesting fact, though, is the word "grow" is translated from the Hebrew word netzer. Netzer is the root of "Nazareth." And He was called a Nazarene.[24]

> *Then he went and settled in a town called Nazareth to fulfill what was spoken through the prophets, that He will be called a Nazarene.*
> ~Matthew 2:23

Back to that blooming rose... At age ten, eagerly anticipating the more familiar carols of the season, I reluctantly allowed myself to learn the words to this new-to-me song. I grew to love it. A more

---

[24] http://mikeblume.com/jan1512.htm, (accessed 4/10/2017)

contemporary song shares the same significance in today's language. Both musical pieces paint expressions of Jesus as the pure and sweet baby boy, born to wear the thorns for you and me.

Grab your magnifying glass and your hound dogs, and let's go sleuthing to learn what links Jesus to this rose. Two mentions of rose appear in the Bible. Solomon's bride gives herself the title, except this flower is believed to be a red tulip (tulipa montana).

> *I am a rose of Sharon, a lily of the valleys.*
> *~Song of Solomon 2:1*

So little help there, we move our investigation forward to the second mention of rose. Isaiah foretells the restoration of Israel with these words

> *The wilderness and the dry land will be glad; the desert will rejoice and blossom like a rose.*
> *~Isaiah 35:1*

Narcissus (narcissus tazetta) receives the honors here. Tulips and jonquils! Where will our great detective minds look next?

> "The Apocryphal books excluded from Scripture by most Christian denominations, do include details of history, beliefs, and culture of their day, shedding additional light on the rose in Biblical times. In II Esdras, written during the first century of the Christian era, Ezra engages in dialogue about the meaning of Israel's sufferings. He describes visions revealing what God will do in the near future on Israel's behalf."[25]

---

[25] Peter Kirby, *Early Jewish Writings*. http://www.earlyjewishwritings.com (accessed 4/10/2017)

> *I will send you help, my servants Isaiah and Jeremiah. According to their counsel I have consecrated and prepared for you twelve trees loaded with various fruits, and the same number of springs flowing with milk and honey, and seven mighty mountains on which roses and lilies grow; by these I will fill your children with joy.*
>
> ~2 Esdras 2:18-19[25]

Whether the stories contained in this extra-Biblical volume are true or simply conjecture, mountains with roses and lilies growing upon them offer hope of renewed joy. "Roses of the mountains" references true rose (Rosa phoenicia and Rosa damascena) growing prolifically on the hillsides of Lebanon, Syria, or Turkey.[26]

This fact, at least culturally, may keep our investigation from landing in the cold case file. They offer a clue to consider why one title Jesus carries is "The Christmas Rose." True roses grew on mountains and symbolized hope and joy. Jesus birth, life, death, and resurrection radiate the hope of joy renewed. Sounds plausible, but truthfully, the answer may lie more in legend than Scripture.

The songs and extra-Biblical findings (and our sniffing hound dogs) draw us to the infant and the cross, the source of amazingly fragrant joy even in the midst of the bleakest situations! An ages old story favors a young girl, Madelon, following the shepherds to Bethlehem. Having no gift to bring, the poor child's tears dropped to the ground producing beautiful roses she presented to the Baby Jesus.[27] Enhanced in the retelling, the legend rooted itself in Jesse's stump.

---

[26] David Stewart, Ph. D., *Healing Oils of the Bible*, (Marble Head, Missouri: Care Publications, 2003) pages 128-130

[27] http://www.worldofchristmas.net/christmas-stories/legend-of-christmas-rose.html, (accessed 4/10/2017)

Roses top favorite flower lists. There are meanings man has attached to each color of roses. The pink color of Rosa damascena represents hope and joy. Red roses represent love. Hope, joy, and love lend ample reason to perceive Jesus as the Christmas Rose.

What is our response as we come into His presence? Like little Madelon, are you saddened that you believe you have no gift to bring? Jesus required only Madelon's heart. Her tears spoke volumes without the roses, but they offered a visible reminder of her belief in the love, hope, and joy she recognized in the tiny baby. He already owned her heart. Does Jesus own your heart? What "roses" do you bring to Him?

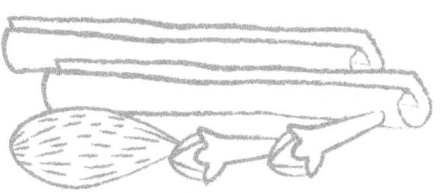

NOTE: Essential oil distillers most commonly produce rose essential oil from the pink Rosa damascena. The highest known electromagnetic frequency of any essential oil - 320 MHz – belongs to Rosa damascena.

> "The effectiveness of essential oils cannot be fully understood without some discussion of frequency. Frequency is the measurable rate of electrical energy flow that is constant between any two points. Everything has frequency. Dr. Robert O. Becker in his book, "The Body Electric," establishes that the human body has an electrical frequency.
> In 1992, Bruce Tainio of Tainio Technology, an independent division of Eastern State University in Cheny, Washington, built the first frequency monitor in the world. Tainio has determined that the average frequency of the human body during the daytime is 62 - 68 Hz. (A healthy body frequency is 62 - 72 Hz.)

Processed/canned food has a frequency of zero. Fresh produce has up to 15 Hz, dried herbs from 12 to 22 Hz and fresh herbs from 20 to 27 Hz. Essential oils start at 52 Hz and go as high as 320 Hz, which is the frequency of rose oil. Clinical research shows that essential oils have the highest frequency of any natural substance known to man."[28]

---

[28] http://www.apteraromatherapy.com/articles4.html, (accessed 4/7/2017).

A Woman of the Bible Experience the Joy of Love

...and Martha Received the Rose

"Like freshly cut roses, I place life in a vase... of love."[29]
~~Kamand Kojouri

Why does she always get the bum rap? Offering the expected hospitality to her guests, with her apron in a wad and sweat dripping from her nose, Martha approached Jesus for help. He presented her a rose instead.

Rose, the queen of flowers, commands a hefty price. One liter of pure rose essential oil contains 3.5 tons (7,000 pounds) of petals. Break that down a bit farther and you'll discover 10,000 roses are required to distill enough oil to fill a single 5 ml bottle — or 833 dozen roses in a bottle the size of your thumb. Hand-picking between dawn and 10 a.m. is crucial for harvesting the roses before essential oils evaporate.[30] Ensuring they arrive at the distillery in pristine condition requires great care.

Color enhances the language of flowers. During harvest, Rosa damascena blankets the hills with flourishes of pink everywhere you look. We've already recognized pink roses represent hope and joy. In flower symbolism they also speak of grace, elegance, admiration, and appreciation.

Jesus is often referred to as a rose. He allowed His life to be broken and poured out for us as a fragrant offering. A popular Christian worship song, *The Rose of Bethlehem* (Lowell Alexander, 1992), interjects thoughts of Him being crushed and broken like we might step on a rose that has fallen on the ground. The crushing release the fragrance.

---

[29] Kamand Kojouri, Quote found on author page on Goodreads. (Used with permission.) https://kamandkojouri.wordpress.com/ (accessed 9/22/2017)

[30] https://www.youtube.com/watch?v=XmRnON4FSUM&feature=youtu.be (accessed 9/22/2017)

Martha loved Jesus, and He loved her! He frequently visited Martha and her brother and sister, Lazarus and Mary, in their home. Several days before the dinner party in question, Martha ran to meet Jesus on the road while Mary stayed behind crying with other mourners. Their brother Lazarus died in spite of their prayers and belief that Jesus would arrive in time to heal him.

The knowledge that He was The Only One to turn to in her hour of need fueled Martha's desperate run into His presence. Her anguished heart fully believed had Jesus arrived sooner He would have saved Lazarus' life. No accusation, just faith that trusted Him before resurrection proof. We hear Martha's words:

> *"Lord, if You had been here, my brother wouldn't have died. Yet even now I know that whatever You ask from God, God will give You."*
>
> ~John 11:21-22

With grace and admiration, Jesus presents Martha with a perfect rose. His words to her became one of the most beloved and cherished Bible passages ever.

> *"I am the resurrection and the life. The one who believes in Me, even if he dies, will live. Everyone who lives and believes in Me will never die—ever. Do you believe this?"*
>
> ~John 11:25-26

Without hesitation, and with limited understanding of events about to unfold, she accepts His fragrant gift, responding perfectly:

> *"Yes, Lord,"* she told Him, *"I believe You are the Messiah, the Son of God, who comes into the world."*
>
> ~John 11:27

What a beautiful scene to witness. Admire the beautiful rose effervescent with aroma - the Message of eternal life, and Martha accepts, believes, and clings to the promise without hesitation. She ran to call her sister, Mary. "The Master is asking for you." Mary joined Jesus and the disciples. At this moment her words to Jesus fell rather flat compared to Martha's.

> *"Lord, if You had been here, my brother would not have died!"*
> ~John 11:32

She began just as Martha did, but Mary's words lacked the faith that transcends time and space. Martha displayed a faith that trusted for the miraculous in spite of the circumstances.

> *The fundamental fact of existence is that this trust in God, this faith, is the firm foundation under everything that makes life worth living. It's our handle on what we can't see. The act of faith is what distinguished our ancestors, set them above the crowd.*
> ~Hebrews 11:1-2 (The Message)

For her faith beyond what she could see, Jesus gifted her a rose — a glimpse of Himself cherished by every generation since. How about you?

> *That is why the LORD says, "Turn to me now, while there is time. Give me your hearts. Come with fasting, weeping, and mourning. Don't tear your clothing in your grief, but tear your hearts instead." Return to the LORD your God, for he is merciful and compassionate, slow to get angry and filled with unfailing love. He is eager to relent and not punish.*
> ~Joel 2:12-13 (NLT)

Have you acknowledged our Rose, Jesus, as the Messiah, the Son of God, and accepted Him and as the Lord of your life. Do you know Him, and believe in your heart — beyond a doubt — He is your only hope for resurrection to eternal life in heaven following your death or at Christ's return? If you would like to choose to follow Jesus today, please pray this prayer.

> *Dear Jesus, the Christmas Rose, I choose today to enter into an intimate relationship with You. I recognize You as the only way to heaven. It's not easy to admit, but I've lived without You far too long. I confess that my life falls way short everyday. I believe You came to live, die, and rise again to forgive my sins and take me to heaven to live with You forever. Today I acknowledge You as the Son of the one true God, and choose to make You the Lord of my life. Amen.*

Let us know your decision. We will pray for you. (Our contact info is in the back of the book.) Then share with a Jesus-following friend the decision you have made today. Attend church with your friend. Or find a Bible-believing church, join a women's small group, or attend a Sunday school class. In this way you will be connected to other women who will hold you accountable to your decision, pray with you, and mentor you in your new walk with Jesus. (If the first church you attend doesn't meet these criteria, attend another. You will find the right one for you.)

NOTE: To those of you who are already believers, please watch for the new believers who enter your fellowship. Take them under your wing. Mentor them in their walks with Jesus. You will both be enriched by the experience.

Rose Essence Droplets

I have told you these things so that you will be filled with my joy. Yes, your joy will overflow! This is my commandment: Love each other in the same way I have loved you.
~John 15:11-12 (NLT)

Fun Facts:

- What we usually call thorns on the rose bush are prickles.[31]
- Rose is the official flower of England. The United States adopted the rose as a national symbol in 1986. Four states, New York, Iowa, North Dakota, and Georgia, also claim the rose as their state flower.[30]
- The largest rose ever grown is a pink rose measuring 33 inches in diameter.[32]
- Cavriglia in Italy boasts the largest private rose garden in the world. I would love to view their 7,500 different rose varieties.[31]
- The Cathedral of Hildesheim in Germany is home to the world's oldest rose plant. Records date it back to 815 A.D. It remained even when the cathedral was destroyed during WWII.[31]
- The Mary Washington Rose was named by George Washington, the first rose breeder in the United States. He named it in honor of his mother.[31]
- The largest ever rose bouquet contained 156,940 roses.[33]

---

[31] http://www.sciencekids.co.nz/sciencefacts/plants/roses.html (accessed 6/20/2017)
[32] http://www.flowerweb.com/en/article/195137/15-Amazing-Facts-about-Roses (accessed 6/20/2017)
[33] https://www.britannica.com/topic/list-of-plants-in-the-family-Rosaceae-2001612 (accessed 6/20/2017)

- The rose family is comprised of over 2500 species, including strawberries, cherries, pears, plums, almonds, and raspberries.[32]

Your Turn:
- A favorite childhood memory was making crepe paper flowers with my grandmother. These are making a comeback. Find instructions for roses at the link below.[34]
- Use petals from your rose garden to make DIY personal care products like Rose Petal and Lavender Sugar Scrub. A recipe for this is in the links below.[35]
- Plant a rose garden. If your space is limited, consider a container rose garden. You will find suggestions for the types of roses and how to do it at the link below.[36]
- The colors of roses are very significant. Do an online search and learn their meanings.

---

[34] https://liagriffith.com/crepe-paper-juliet-roses/ (accessed 6/21/2017)
[35] http://www.bydreamsfactory.com/2016/10/diy-rose-petal-lavender-sugar-scrub.html/ (accessed 6/21/2017)
[36] http://balconygardenweb.com/small-rose-garden-growing-roses-in-containers-balcony-patio-and-terrace/ (accessed 6/21/2017)

Chapter 5

Mint
The Joy of Giving

Cinnamah-Brosia and Friends Share About

Mint – The Joy of Giving

Diffusing Today: Peppermint, of course
Aromatic Influence: Creates an atmosphere that may be calming yet stimulating and uplifting
Daily Delight: Mint Chocolate Brownies
Musically: **Little Drummer Boy**
Verse of the Day:
> Each person should do as he has decided in his heart—
> not reluctantly or out of necessity, for God loves a cheerful giver.
> ~~2 Corinthians 9:7

Just a few weeks ago our Tuesday night group discussed our traditional Christmas party. "We always draw names. We'll do that again this year, right?" Melanie asked. While she totally got into the whole gift giving tradition, some of the others in the group were groaning over the annual obligatory exchange of stuff. Haley quietly surfed around on her phone. Her lack of consideration aside, she found and shared this quote from E.B. White:

> "To perceive Christmas through its wrapping
> becomes more difficult with every year."[37]

We all knew the Christmas story, and acknowledged it made sense putting less focus on things. Often the gifts spoke highly of another item checked off our shopping list, rather than a gift from our heart. Carol suggested creativity. We encouraged a $20 limit. Haley remained visibly uncomfortable. We drew names anyway and planned the party.

Tonight we were gathered in Sophia's Corner. The area glowed with the lights and festive sparkles of Kaitlyn's gift for turning an

---

[37] E.B. White, *The Distant Music of the Hounds*, 1954, found at http://www.azquotes.com/quote/313012, (accessed 9/15/2017)

ordinary corner into a festive wonderland. We piled many versions of heavenly chocolate delights and sugary confections on the upcycled pomegranate bordered coffee table. Shimmery red liquid cascaded from the punch fountain. The coffee urn wafted its aroma.

Mandy's beautiful voice led us in worship to the King whose birthday gave us reason to celebrate. Jane shared a moving devotion about using the gifts God has given us. "It's easy to discard them or be ungrateful for the gifts He has personally chosen for you and me. Finding joy in these gifts prompts us to serve in authenticity and love. Your actions please Your Lord."

We love because He first loved us.
~1 John 4:19

She prayed, "Oh, LORD, help us find joy in the gifts you have chosen for each of us. We also choose joy in the gifts we bring for our friends and those they chose for us. Let us leave here deeper in love with You and each other. In Jesus' Name, Amen."

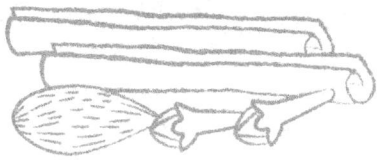

Beginning with Crystal, we revealed whose name we held and presented our gifts. Jennifer loved adding another warm scarf to her collection, and hugged Crystal in thanks. The green and white striped package boasted a blown glass Christmas tree ornament tied to the top. Melanie handed it with great care to Carol. Inside she discovered three more glass jewels to add to her special glass themed tree. Another big hug, and around the circle we went. Haley and I were the only ones left. It thrilled me when I drew her name. Now I realized she had mine, too.

The red and white polka dot box pulled me in. I quickly recognized it as a work of art. Not to disturb the beauty of the wrapping, the lid lifted separately. Tears ran from my eyes as I opened it. More red and white polka dot paper – so reminiscent of the dishes at Miss Dot's Café – peered up at me. Each one held a photo memory of Miss Dot's Café and all the people who made it special over the years. What a perfect gift!

Curiosity won. I inquired, "Where did you find all these photos?" Haley pointed to Carol.

"Mom had taken these over all the years she and Miss Dot were friends. I knew Haley desired so much to bring you an extra-special gift – one that shared her heart. You and Jeremy mean so much to Haley and Dan. Mom agreed the photos belonged here at The Coffee Cottage. Haley did all the work to make them come to life with her special touches, captions, and more." It was 'that one gift' that made everyone wish they had been so creative.

What a tough act to follow! I handed Haley her gift and impatiently awaited the surprise she would find inside. At The Coffee Cottage we still use what remains of the polka dot dishes, and Haley absolutely loves them. Hidden in the white oval basket overflowing with a stash of Haley's favorite wild red raspberry tea, I had nested two of the polka dot cups. The glittery gold bow reminded me of how much I treasure our friendship. Haley squealed with delight. I jotted a mental note to thank Jeremy for the awesome idea.

The photo box remains at The Cottage for everyone to enjoy. As the party ended, our hearts were filled with the love of the Baby lying in the manger over 2000 years ago. We always leave a seat for Jesus when we meet. Tonight was no exception. We finished with a chorus of the traditional birthday song in His honor.

The Essence of Mint in Scripture

The Mint of Legalism

Botanical Name: Mentha longifolia; native to the Middle East

Caught up to the pinnacle in their legalism and exacting obedience to the jots and tittles of the law, the Pharisees tithed everything, and very precisely. They brought their gift to God's temple as the Law (and their added laws) directed. They awaited a Messiah. Even though He stood right before their eyes, they failed to recognize the One their gift was meant to honor.

> *"Woe to you, scribes and Pharisees, hypocrites! For you tithe mint and dill and cumin, and have neglected the weightier provisions of the law: justice and mercy and faithfulness; but these are the things you should have done without neglecting the others."*
> ~Matthew 23:23 (NASB)

Jesus rebuked the Pharisees for playing church. He called them out for tithing their mint, dill, and cumin, while remaining blind to their spiritual condition. They traipsed their merry way through life with little thought for real sacrifice. Hauled in by the bushels, their tithe appeared enormous. Considering the rapidly spreading growth habits of this herb, there was plenty more where it came from. They sure did look good in their own eyes, adding stars to their holier-than-Thou attitudes. Jesus looked right through their transparent façade.

Mint is prominent in our culture, with peppermint candy canes leading the holiday mint brigade. Seeing one immediately transports our thoughts to Christmas. Legend claims in 1670 a choirmaster in Cologne, Germany requested plain white sticks of sugar candy from a local candy maker. He hoped to keep children quiet during the living crèche. Red stripes were eventually added and one end bent to represent Jesus' shepherd staff or His monogram. The red stripes call attention to the blood He shed for all mankind. From history rather than legend, we learn candy canes as we know them today, were first made in Albany, Georgia in the 1920s;[38] but the sweet stories surrounding them point us to Jesus. The Pharisees could have used the example.

Lacking explanation, mint originally (and still most often) flavored the candy novelty. Peppermint extract is derived from the leaves of the invasive mint plant. Rhizomes creep along the ground creating new plants, spreading wildly through the garden space, assuring a bumper crop. This prolific herb boasts an array of benefits. Among them, it may be cooling to the skin, and is potentially helpful in supporting digestion. Many agree it tastes amazing too. Yet, mint is mentioned only once in the Bible, and it is cheap!

So, the Pharisees gift cost them very little, and it showed no love for Jesus in their hearts. They brought in the full 10% of their mint, dill, and cumin, but their hearts remained far from a relationship with God the Father or with Jesus. They were throwing in the prolific overgrowth that may have been potential waste anyway. Jesus' gift to His followers represented eternal forethought from the heart of the Father. Their tithe cost them nothing. Jesus' gift would cost the Father the life of His only Son.

About our own gifts, Jesus reminds us:

> *"Don't collect for yourselves treasures on earth, where moth and rust destroy and where thieves break in and steal. But collect for yourselves treasures in heaven, where neither moth nor rust destroys, and where thieves don't break in and steal. For where your treasure is, there your heart will be also."*
>
> ~Matthew 6:19-21

---

[38] https://www.cbsnews.com/news/the-history-of-candy-canes/ (accessed 9/22/2017)

A Woman of the Bible Experience the Joy of Giving

She Gave Everything She Had
She Gave Her Whole Life

If instead of a gem, or even a flower, we should cast the gift of a loving thought into the heart of a friend, that would be giving as the angels give.[39] ~George MacDonald

There was no gift in the world I desired more for my thirteenth birthday. Transistor radios ran on a 9-Volt battery, fit in your pocket, and picked up great AM stations back in the 1960s when I was a teenager. I begged incessantly. Even though under $10, they were pricey according to the economy of the day. My parents' efforts to encourage a different choice failed miserably. Mom worked extra shifts at her retail job so my dream could come true. On my big day, I received the desire of my heart. I enjoyed my portable music, but the satisfaction I felt when listening to that little treasure box was always tarnished by the thoughts of mom's sacrifice — and to tell the truth, it was a cheaper version and never worked very well. But it was a gift of love that cost her much.

In stark contrast to the Pharisees' gifts, Jesus made a point to single out a very special lady who literally gave her last dime. It was all she had left of whatever life may have been for her before. And she gave it from her heart.

> *Sitting across from the offering box, he was observing how the crowd tossed money in for the collection. Many of the rich were making large contributions. One poor widow came up and put in two small coins—a measly two cents. Jesus called his disciples over and said, "The truth is that this poor widow gave more to the collection*

---

[39] John MacDonald, *The Complete Novels of John MacDonald*, quote found at https://www.brainyquote.com/quotes/quotes/g/georgemacd105245.html (accessed 9/15/2017)

> *than all the others put together. All the others gave what they'll never miss; she gave extravagantly what she couldn't afford—she gave her all."*
> ~~Mark 12:41-44 (The Message)

We didn't sacrifice food to eat or a roof over our heads, but all these years later I'm reminded of Mom's sacrifice for me. She loved me in spite of my bratty-ness and sacrificed her time and energy because of her love. Retail salaries in the 1960s were low. To make my wish come true took no telling how many extra hours on her feet – feet that often ached miserably without any added strain. The gift presented by the woman Jesus spoke of carried an even steeper price tag.

Imagine, if you can, giving absolutely everything you have. All of our lives consist of way more than she could begin to comprehend. She had no husband. She had no money. Probably she had no home. She could have been living on the street and would most likely starve if she gave those last two coins. She was still breathing, of course, but it's like she gave her whole life – at least all that was left of it.

Contrary to popular beliefs today, first century men and women sat at the feet of their rabbi as they taught from the Torah. This happened in homes and in the temple court, an area well-connected to everyday Jewish life. If she had no home, perhaps she spent much time at the temple in the presence of Jesus and His disciples, witnessing something different in the living of their lives that made her willing to lay it all down for her Lord. Something touched her, because Jesus makes it clear she gave it out of love and devotion. What she gave were not a few measly leaves from her uber-abundant harvest. Others did that. And for all the wrong reasons. What she saw in His life awakened a fire in her spirit that could not be quenched by her circumstances. Jesus honored her for it. He made her motives (and theirs) known for the rest of time.

What constitutes your whole life? Money, and what else? Certainly time, talents, gifts, abilities, dreams, passions, desires, pleasures, pastimes, possessions, business, children, spouse, friends, extended family, home, leisure, and food make the list. What would you add?

Personal pleasures are part of our lives. I believe God desires for us to enjoy them as long as we do not dishonor Him in the process. He created so many wonderful things to delight us, He must be pleased when we find joy in them. The bigger question here is: Do we become too obsessed with the diversions to hear God's voice when He asks us to sacrifice our time, our comfort, and our treasures to help someone else? You may willingly make sacrifices for your children like my mother did, but is your life open to giving whatever He asks?

The widow we visited responded to the call, giving her very last two cents, leaving her with nothing. And we already know she did it joyfully. How do we do that? A portion of this devotion comes from a Bible study lesson I wrote and shared many years ago – long before Pinterest. I've seen the same idea I'm about to share featured there now, but it was an inspired moment for me at the time. I found note cards shaped like purses. The cards opened to expose an area for the message. I glued two pennies to the blank space and wrote the words "She gave everything she had. She gave her whole life." These were distributed as a reminder to each lady in the study.

With all the beautiful scrapbook papers out there today, you can easily use the pattern below to create a purse like this. Make it look tattered, or decorate it elaborately. (Maybe it was all she had left of what was once a much different life.) Treasure it as a reminder the essence of joy is found in freely giving out of the richness of your love for Jesus.

She gave everything she had. She gave her whole life.

Mint Essence Droplets

Each person should do as he has decided in his heart—not reluctantly or out of necessity, for God loves a cheerful giver.
2 Corinthians 9:7

Fun Facts:
- Mint is a member of the Lamiaceae or deadnettle family of plants, which also includes basil, rosemary, sage, savory, marjoram, oregano, hyssop, thyme, and lavender.[40]
- Peppermint is a hybrid of spearmint and water mint.[41]
- Peppermint was mentioned in Icelandic Pharmacopoeias beginning in 1240 A.D. The London Pharmacopoeia of 1721 also included mint.[42]
- Native Americans grew varieties of mint and were aware of their importance before European settlers arrived.[41]
- 90% of the 1.75 billion candy canes made each year are purchased between Thanksgiving and Christmas.
- December 26 is National Candy Cane Day.[42]
- A pastry chef in Geneva, Alain Roby, is in the book of world records for producing the world's longest candy cane. It measured 51 feet long. (Some sources claim 63 feet).[44]
- Almost 70% of the world's mint supply is grown in the United States.[45]

---

[40] https://en.m.wikipedia.org/wiki/Lamiaceae (accessed 9/15/2017)
[41] https://en.m.wikipedia.org/wiki/Peppermint (accessed 9/15/2017)
[42] http://peppermint.indepthinfo.com/history-of-peppermint (accessed 9/15/2017)
[43] https://www.gourmetgiftbaskets.com/Blog/post/candy-cane-facts.aspx (accessed 9/16/2017)
[44] http://www.dailyherald.com/article/20121207/news/712079523/ (accessed 9/16/2017)
[45] https://wisagclassroom.org/wp-content/uploads/2016/04/Mint-Fact-Sheet.pdf (accessed 9/16/2017)

- Dried peppermint leaves are among the many herbs and essential oils found in Egyptian tombs.[46]
- Dr. Ephraim K. Smith photographed old barns in Michigan. He happened upon an abandoned peppermint mill. His discovery led him to produce a documentary on the history of peppermint growers in the United States.[45]

Your Turn:
- Use crushed peppermint and peppermint sticks or candy canes to enhance your hot chocolate or eggnog. Here are recipes: Peppermint Eggnog Milkshake[47] or Mint Hot Cocoa[48]
- Make your own Peppermint Extract[49] or Peppermint Syrup[48]
- Keep a journal of the gifts you give and receive during the coming year. Which ones mean the most? How did forethought play into the significance of the gift?
- Use the pattern included with "The Woman Who Gave Everything" devotion to make paper purses with your family or small group. Keep them as a reminder of giving from the heart. Discuss ways to be a more cheerful giver.
- We have found simple, cute, inexpensive, yet thoughtful minty gift ideas for you to create. Find them on our Pinterest Board: The Essence of Joy.[50]

---

[46] http://herbs.lovetoknow.com/History_of_Peppermint (accessed 9/16/2017)

[47] http://www.momontimeout.com/2013/11/peppermint-eggnog-milkshake/ (accessed 9/16/2017)

[48] http://www.myfrugalhome.com/how-to-make-peppermint-extract/ (accessed 9/16/2017)

[49] http://cookingwithcurls.com/2016/01/09/peppermint-syrup/ (accessed 9/16/2017)

[50] https://www.pinterest.com/lynnuwatson/the-essence-of-joy/ (accessed 9/22/2017)

Chapter 6

Fig
The Joy of Security

Cinnamon-Brosia and Friends Share About
Fig – The Joy of Security

Diffusing Today: Lavender and Bergamot (citrus family) essential oils
Aromatic Influence: Helps to create an atmosphere filled with feelings of love and security
Daily Delight: Fig Cookies
Musically: ***Born to Die*** (Bebo Norman)
Verse of the Day:
> *Protect me, God, for the only safety I know*
> *is found in the moments I seek You.*
> Psalm 16:1 (VOICE)

Someone finding a quiet corner to be alone with their latte happens often at Cinnamah-Brosia's Coffee Cottage. Today was Eileen's turn. Jane spotted her pain and served the newcomer her beverage. Allowing her space for an extended time, Jane returned and asked if she needed to talk. In tears, Eileen poured it all out.

"Claire behaved in unhealthy ways toward Sam from the beginning of their relationship. Her disdain for me regularly punched the air from my lungs. The obvious darkness of this girl's life built walls between Sam and his brother, Henry, too.

"She despised the Jesus talk in our home and demanded Sam get away from it all. Henry, begged him over and over to trust Jesus and leave this all behind. Spellbound by her influence, Sam refused over and over again. Last weekend was the last straw. The discord continued right up to Henry and Maddie's wedding day — a day devoted to promised love and faithfulness. Claire's skill at manipulation caused Sam to show up just 10 minutes before the wedding. Henry counted on him to be his best man. Sam stood in the line, but another friend fulfilled the duties. Big fights ensued, while we attempted to keep the drama hidden from our guests.

"Sam disappeared immediately after the wedding. Both boys lived at home until then. Today Sam packed his things and moved in with Claire's family. Apparently, sleeping on a cot in their detached garage with no plumbing dangled a carrot too alluring to pass up. In his mind, at least he was away from all of us and from our religion. Suddenly we occupied an empty nest, too! I am so angry, and I can't believe I just shared this all with you, a perfect stranger. I should be going. Please don't think badly of me."

Jane touched her arm gently and offered an understanding look. "May I share a story before you go?"

Eileen nodded, and Jane began. "His girlfriend worshipped him — a little too much. Maybe a whole lot too much. She also controlled him, driving a wedge that severed relationships with every member of Andrea's family. Living through the ordeal left deep scars. Andrea is my husband's sister. Her son, Chad, made similar choices to Sam. His father, Curt; brother, Brandon; and his mom hurt terribly.

"Several months went by when Chad realized his new choice of 'home and family' fell far short of his expectations. The girl's parents demanded rent he could barely afford to occupy a spot on the sofa in their basement. Family meals consisted of hotdogs, potato chips, and coke. Occasionally the shelf contained a box of dry cereal. Most mornings he bought an egg biscuit on his way to work. Party time every night took its toll. Then he lost his job. His efforts to leave the situation produced anger and threats from the girl.

"When he finally reached out to his dad, Curt arrived with the police and escorted him home. Swallowing truckloads of pride he admitted he believed God abandoned him. Having been so sure of his moves, he realized his cupboards were bare, he had no place worth laying his head, and he had been used and abused in so many ways. Andrea and Curt allowed him to return home for a time. Well aware he was an adult, they still insisted on some ground rules. One of those – he would attend church with them. Quiet time with God was most important to Curt and Andrea. They prayed their example would inspire him to begin doing that, too. He enrolled in a trade school. Found new friends. One step at a time they all liked each other again. Today he owns a highly reputable auto repair shop, he married a girl the whole family adores, they have two little girls, and all of them love Jesus. By the way Sierra and Madison are the delights of Andrea's life!

"Listening to you caused me to relive those moments in the life of our extended family. In the times when we felt so empty inside, the idea of praying, much less praising God in our lack appeared impossible. May I pray for you and your family?"

Eileen agreed. Jane took Eileen's hand in hers and spent several minutes quietly asking God to calm Eileen's spirit, and to bring restoration to their family.

Jane added this thought after the prayer. "Our family believes God allowed this to happen for all of us to encourage others. Andrea, Curt, and Chad love for their story to bring glimpses of God's redemption, empowering others to trust He cares and works on their behalf even when it looks impossible.

"Andrea, Curt, and our extended family prayed day and night to see change in their son's life. God heard their prayers and answered in His perfect timing."

For those praying like this for a loved one, do not lose heart. God sees and hears. If you are the "Chad" or the "Sam" in this story, someone may be praying fervently for you as well – praying that you will regret the insecurity created by your rebellion and return to the open arms of God and family. I pray for all of you in this position, that the Holy Spirit will lead your loved one or you back to the place of security and love of Jesus and family. What a joyful reunion!

The Essence of Fig in Scripture

Did Adam and Eve Really Find Security in a Fig Leaf?

Botanical Name: Ficus carica;
native to southwest Asia and the Mediterranean

WOWZER! Just attempt to write a book on joy, and the enemy uses everyone and every circumstance, working overtime to steal every ounce of your heart's treasure box and bring on the worry warts. The tests keep coming and coming! Lessons demand to be learned. Opportunities abound to display the qualities of a good fig rather than a bad one.

Our enemy, the devil, thrives on using tests to steal our joy! You know those joy-crushers poking around in your business. A blog post on Beliefnet[51] suggests these:

- Complaining
- Procrastination
- Gossip
- Approval seeking
- Not keeping your word
- Unkindness
- Attachment to circumstances
- Living in the past
- Fear of the future
- Thanklessness
- Chaos
- Jealousy
- Disconnected from people
- Insecurities

---

[51] http://www.beliefnet.com/inspiration/articles/simple-ways-to-have-joy.aspx (accessed 9/20/2017)

Before you dismiss this as a do-gooder, holier-than-thou, super spiritual list, realize this reflects the secular world's list of joy-crushers; the spiritual and the not-so-spiritual echo the same truths and challenges. How often when succumbing to one of these do the others play Follow-the-Leader? We're quickly shoved into overwhelmed-gear, destitute of hope and joy. And then we worry about everything?

Jesus came to make our lives full rather than wallowing in our insecurities and discontentment.

> *A thief is only there to steal and kill and destroy. I came so they can have real and eternal life, more and better life than they ever dreamed of.*
> ~John 10:10 (The Message)

That thief came to God's inaugural garden. He stole the hopes and dreams of Adam and Eve, leaving behind counterfeit seeds sown to sin's folly. Many Hebrew scholars claim the fruit was from a fig tree. It may or may not be true, but Adam and Eve did choose the leaves of the fig tree to cover their nakedness. They further hid themselves among the tree. Fig leaves are very large - up to 7" by 10" in size with a sticky coating on the underside. An effective canopy, but imagine the discomfort of humanity's first clothing fad.

> *Now the woman saw that the tree was good for food, and that it was a thing of lust for the eyes, and that the tree was desirable for imparting wisdom. So she took of its fruit and she ate. She also gave to her husband who was with her and he ate. Then the eyes of both of them were opened and they knew that they were naked; so they sewed fig leaves together and made for themselves loin-coverings. And they heard the sound of Adonai Elohim going to and fro in the garden in the wind of the day. So the man and his wife hid themselves from the presence of Adonai Elohim in the midst of the Tree of the garden.*
> ~Genesis 3:6-8 (TLV)

We find the fig tree well beyond the Garden of Eden. A quick word search on a Bible app reveals fig trees' importance throughout the Bible, often used in reference to security and abundance or lack thereof. When the trees represent God's people, we most often note the people's choice to complain about their plight. They may chase other gods, fail to trust God in challenging circumstances, or fear the future. They may promote and honor self and nurture friendships with the wrong crowd. In these circumstances it becomes easy to abandon prayerfulness. What a reflection of the universal list of the joy-crushers.

God shows Jeremiah (Chapter 24) baskets of good figs and bad figs, asking him what he sees. Jeremiah sees figs, while God sees His people who live their lives for Him versus those who have gone after other pleasures and other gods.

Habakkuk begins his short book complaining of all the injustices his people face, taking his arguments to the Almighty. He asks, "Why, God?" God reveals the answer to him through a vision anything but encouraging. The situation worsens for his countrymen. Habakkuk finds himself convinced God simply doesn't care. Where's the good life He promised? Where's His power to change the circumstances? Where is His compassion?

God's response expresses His justice. He expresses His loving kindnesses to the faithful. In disciplining the unfaithful, however, many are affected. Through it all, God has the big picture. As his short book comes to an end, Habakkuk reminds himself and his readers the authentic good life develops through trusting God and rejoicing in His love and care in spite of appearances. Real security and abundance are found in hearts filled with the joy of the Spirit.

> *Though the fig tree does not bud and there is no fruit on the vines, though the olive crop fails and the fields produce no food, though there are no sheep in the pen and no cattle in the stalls, yet I will triumph in Yahweh; I will rejoice in the God of my salvation! Yahweh my Lord is my strength; He makes my feet like those of a deer and enables me to walk on mountain heights!*
>
> ~Habakkuk 3:17-19

Jesus walked the rounds of suffering and much less than desirable circumstances. He faced undeserved attacks on His character because of the wrongful actions of many. Facing difficulties and suffering ourselves, we often believe 'I'm the only one,' then whine, complain, and lose our joy. Jesus never did. One of His lessons on the topic included a fig tree. One producing no fruit withered at His command.

> *Early in the morning, as He was returning to the city, He was hungry. Seeing a lone fig tree by the road, He went up to it and found nothing on it except leaves. And He said to it, "May no fruit ever come from you again!" At once the fig tree withered. When the disciples saw it, they were amazed and said, "How did the fig tree wither so quickly?" Jesus answered them, "I assure you: If you have faith and do not doubt, you will not only do what was done to the fig tree, but even if you tell this mountain, 'Be lifted up and thrown into the sea,' it will be done. And if you believe, you will receive whatever you ask for in prayer."*
> ~Matthew 21:18-22

When even momentarily we lose our joy, 'withered' proves a great description of our spiritual, mental, and perhaps even our physical state. Finding our security and abundance in Him instead of our circumstances keeps us fresh with joy. Our lives provide inspiration and blessing to others. Our contentment brings glory to God. We find our home in the basket of good figs.

> *"A good tree doesn't produce bad fruit; on the other hand, a bad tree doesn't produce good fruit. For each tree is known by its own fruit. Figs aren't gathered from thornbushes, or grapes picked from a bramble bush. A good man produces good out of the good storeroom of his heart. An evil man produces evil out of the evil storeroom, for his mouth speaks from the overflow of the heart.*
> ~Luke 6:43-45

What steals your joy? What circumstances make you wither? Do you quickly seek Jesus? Do you give Him lip service, but allow your discontent to rot your figs on the tree? Do you just let your fruit fall to the ground to be stomped? Where do you turn to restore your joy? Do you quickly realize your abundant security in the "God is all we need" form of enough?

A Woman of the Bible Who Experiences the Joy of Security
The Widow's Never-Ending Oil Supply

Joy . . . is the reverse of happiness.
Happiness is the result of what happens of an agreeable sort.
Joy has its springs deep down inside.
And that spring never runs dry, no matter what happens.
Only Jesus gives that joy.
He had joy, singing its music within,
even under the shadow of the cross.[52]
S.D. Gordon

"So, bring us some figgy pudding."[53] Christmas carolers rarely offer their festive repertoire without singing We Wish You a Merry Christmas. The holiday season resounds with the familiar and joyful carol, but have you tasted figgy pudding? Fig newtons, perhaps, but figgy pudding?

The original recipe called for thirteen ingredients. Christian symbolism suggest they represent Jesus and His twelve apostles. The holly sprig on top stood as a reminder of Jesus suffering at His crucifixion.[54]

The fruit of the fig tree visibly appears several times a year, while masses of flower buds are tucked inside the fruit. Pollination occurs when a wasp specific to the genus bores its way into the intimate hideaway depositing eggs on the female flowers and gathering pollen from the male flowers. In its entirety the process

---

[52] S.D. Gordon, Quote found at: https://www.christianquotes.info/quotes-by-author/s-d-gordon-quotes/#axzz4srdh3loy (accessed 9/16/2017)
[53] https://en.m.wikipedia.org/wiki/We_Wish_You_a_Merry_Christmas (accessed 7/21/2017)
[54] https://www.thespruce.com/figgy-pudding-recipe-1807216 (accessed 7/21/2017)

presents an intricate masterpiece of Divine details. Learn more about the pollination of figs at the link below.[55]

The Divine Creator of all nature's complexities inspired the writers of the Bible to include many references to figs. Let's visit a special lady who lacked security in her circumstances. While we spend time with her, we discover the benefits of being good figs, living in relationship with Jesus and exuding joy in our inner and outer being. Joy grows in the hidden places. It displays fruit even under harsh circumstances — like the way figs are pollinated in the secret place inside the fruit.

Traveling through the pages of Scripture, we hop a ride with the prophet Elijah. We move quickly, because he is running to get away from evil Jezebel and King Ahab. We find shelter, protection, and a miraculous provision at the home of a widow in the heathen country of Zarephath. We witness her forming her last handful of grain and few drops of remaining oil into a cake. She and her son prepare to eat their last meal and die.

Severe famine had overtaken the land, and Elijah had the nerve to show up on her doorstep asking for a meal and shelter. He assures her, her personal supplies will last as long as she needs them. We watch, thinking to ourselves, "Is he crazy or what? There are no provisions here."

But she calls him "man of God." What about Elijah's conversation with the woman impressed her to believe him and invite him in? Was hospitality expected in spite of circumstances? Or did the deed spill from her kind heart, as she chose to share even the last morsel she had?

We witness an amazing miracle of continued provision. After serving us, this 'good fig' continued to provide for Elijah for the next few years. She learned to trust God for her needs in the midst of a sea of unbelief all around her. She experienced God's work up close and personal over the following years.

---

[55] http://www.figweb.org/Interaction/How_do_fig_wasps_pollinate/ (accessed 7/21/2017)

That didn't mean all was perfect. Food shortages no longer plagued her, but she experienced other major challenges. Her son, interacted with and learned from Elijah, bolstering her family's faith. But when her son dies unexpectedly from unknown causes, she questioned the whys: Why God allowed him to live through the famine and now took him away; Why God held her sin against her and punished her; Why, why, why? Habakkuk had done the same thing. Being honest with ourselves, we often react the same way.

How easy to groan and complain rather than acknowledge God's continuous abundance in our lives — rather than allowing our joy to shine through.

Once again God showered her with His blessing. Elijah asked her for her son to be brought to him. Remembering His earlier faithfulness, she placed the boy in Elijah's arms. Don't you wonder what thoughts traipsed through her mind while Elijah took the boy away to his own room? I know I would be reluctant. She released him to Elijah.

Her son restored to life, she joyfully proclaims:

> *Then the woman said to Elijah, "Now I know you are a man of God and the Lord's word from your mouth is true.*
>
> ~1 Kings 17:24

We were a young couple with a young family. The economy was depressed affecting my husband's job and income. How well I remember often thinking, "Where will our next meal come from?" Our family never went hungry. We called God's miraculous way of producing yet one more meal out of a barren storehouse, "God's magic refrigerator." Of course, there was no magic — only His bounty stored in secret places revealed in God's perfect timing.

The widow learned to trust and find her security in the Lord and His Words. In the same way, our incredibly lean years taught us to be content in our circumstances. We also learned where to place our trust when we walk through seasons of need. We praised Him again and again, secure in knowing 'He had this.' The Apostle, Paul, said it like this:

I have learned to be content in whatever circumstances I am. I know both how to have a little, and I know how to have a lot. In any and all circumstances I have learned the secret of being content—whether well fed or hungry, whether in abundance or in need. I am able to do all things through Him who strengthens me.
~Philippians 4:11b-13

In what difficult situation do you find yourself today? Are you learning to trust in the security Jesus extends to you? Are you learning that He is enough? Do you rejoice even in the uncertainties, believing that He is all you need? Believing He will make the oil and meal last as long as needed? Believing He can redeem impossible situations?

When you do, you leave the people around you wondering why you're joy faucets are wide open when the facts indicate reason to groan and weep instead. They'll ask you why, and you testify to the truth of the Lord!

Fig Essence Droplets

I love you, LORD, you are my strength.
The LORD is my rock, my fortress, and my savior;
my God is my rock, in whom I find protection.
He is my shield, the power that saves me, and my place of safety.
I called on the LORD, who is worthy of praise,
and he saved me from my enemies.
~Psalm 18:1-3 (NLT)

Fun Facts:
- Fig trees were brought to the east coast of the New World in the 1500's by Spanish and Portuguese missionaries. (That included the West Indies and east coast of what is now the United States.) Spanish missionaries took them to California in 1769.[56]
- Figs were a training food for the earliest Olympic athletes.[57]
- A whole fig and 1/2 cup of milk have about the same amount of calcium.[56]
- Fig trees' blossoms are inside of the fruit, and give it its crunchy seed texture when the fruit is fully ripened.[56]
- Figs are the sweetest of all fruits with a 55% sugar content.[58]
- Figs may be substituted for fat in many recipes. Use about 1/2 as much fig as fat the recipe calls for.[57]

---

[56] http://www.cal-ipc.org/ip/management/ipcw/pages/detailreport.cfm@usernumber=50&surveynumber=182.php (accessed 6/21/2017)
[57] http://www.cal-ipc.org/ip/management/ipcw/pages/detailreport.cfm@usernumber=50&surveynumber=182.php (accessed 6/21/2017)
[58] http://www.valleyfig.com/about-our-figs/fig-facts (accessed 6/2/2017

Your Turn:
- Figs are very versatile fruit and may be eaten in numerous ways. The link below offers you 27 different suggestions.[59]
- Grow a fig tree in your back yard. Harvest the bounty.[60]
- Some fig varieties also make wonderful house plants. Choose and cultivate one of them in your home.[61]

---

[59] http://www.huffingtonpost.com/self/fun-facts-about-figs_b_5652557.html (accessed 6/21/2017)

[60] https://www.buzzfeed.com/christinebyrne/delicious-fig-recipes-for-every-occasion?utm_term=.aj81oQppg#.fqVongYY2 (accessed 6/21/2017)

[61] http://www.southernliving.com/home-garden/gardens/how-to-grow-fig-trees (accessed 9/23/2017)

Chapter 7

Cinnamon
The Joy of Integrity

Cinnamah-Brosia and Friends Share About
Cinnamon – The Joy of Integrity

Diffusing Today: Cinnamon and Orange essential oils
Aromatic Influence: Helps fill the environment with a sense of abundant joy
Daily Delight: Snickerdoodles
Musically: ***O Little Town of Bethlehem***
Verse of the Day:
> *"Yes, indeed—God is my salvation. I trust, I won't be afraid. God—yes God!—is my strength and song, best of all, my salvation!" Joyfully you'll pull up buckets of water from the wells of salvation.*
> ~~Isaiah 12:2-3 (The Message)

When you're twelve and "everybody's doing it" holding on to personal integrity rarely becomes a concern. Pastor Gary's wife, Pam, dropped by The Coffee Cottage today. She, Jane, Kaitlyn, and I chatted with concern about the Carley! concert held in a nearby city a few weeks ago. Pre-teen girls think she's amazing, and many of the local girls (including several from church) attended. Pam's youngest, twelve-year-old Laney, did not.

"Well aware of our stand on this, Laney begged and pleaded to go. 'But, Mom, everyone is going.' One mom even offered tickets for Laney and I to attend, and she suggested we take our girls shopping for some Carley! outfits for them to wear to the event. How do you even respond to that? I declined her offer. I asked her the same question we ask of our children and ourselves.

"Would you be embarrassed in that situation or wearing those clothes or listening to that music or watching that movie if Jesus walked into the room?"

"Phrasing it like that," Kaitlyn responded, "puts things in a much different perspective than just 'knowing Jesus is everywhere.'"

"You would think, but the question didn't set well with the mom. I'd rather be a prude with my integrity intact and honor God in my life, than show no discretion about mine or my child's choice of entertainment.

"Together with Laney we checked out the lyrics of Carley! songs, and agreed to their inappropriateness for any one of any age. How could we fill our minds with vulgarity and offensive language and feel good if Jesus sat down next to us? Laney resigned herself to the fact her friends would attend without her. She could attempt to explain why to her friends or make us the bad guys. My conversation with the one mom vividly etched in my memory, I encouraged the latter. She took the first route, and of course, they laughed and made sure she heard them call her the goody-two-shoes-preacher's-kid and worse. She even received suggestions she sneak out and go to prove she was their friend."

"Oh Pam, you made the right decision. But I hurt for Laney. Preteens desire desperately to be accepted, but deep down they want to do the right thing, too. The rejection from her 'friends' wounded her, I know," Jane said.

Pam replied, "So many of the girls are wearing provocative clothing at such a young age. Laney admitted a couple of the girls have experimented with drugs, and they talk about doing things with boys. I find it so sad to be having these deep conversations with such a young girl. Laney, herself, realized the lyrics of the songs, and the clothes Carley! wears convince girls her age to do the same 'cause it's cool. No one pays attention to the consequences. Her awareness made my heart leap for joy."

Jane inquired, "Wasn't there some trouble at the concert? Were Laney's friends involved?"

"We're heartbroken about that. A large group of young kids brought drugs. A couple of Laney's friends were in on it. The parents had no idea. They were pretty much in denial that their children participated. Admission would definitely make them look like bad parents." Pam responded.

C-B interjected, "Proverbs 21:21 comes to mind right now – one of Gram's favorites. I love the VOICE version of it:

> 'Whoever pursues justice and treats others with kindness discovers true life marked by integrity and respect.'"

Just then Laney walked into The Coffee Cottage accompanied by her friend, Carson and Carson's mom. Difficult to disguise, surprise registered on Pam's face.

"I apologized to Laney today," Carson began. "When she told me she wouldn't be going to the concert, she asked me that question, 'What if Jesus was in the room?' I laughed at her 'til my sides hurt. Why did Jesus care anyway, I thought. Of course, the truth of the question stung. I never imagined being offered the drugs and using them. I looked on Carley! as a fun girl. I thought it would be cool to be popular just like her. Her songs make many things appear totally OK! I didn't think anything like this would happen."

Carson's mom added, "Pam, please forgive me for acting so foolish when you turned me down on the tickets. I think I just wanted to be the cool mom in the group. Didn't turn out so cool after all. Now Carson will be doing community service. The choice you and Laney made saved her that embarrassment."

Laney spoke up. "Mom, I think some of my friends would like to learn to make better decisions. I want them to know Jesus, too. I knew you would be here with Cinnamah, Kaitlyn, and Miss Jane. So, we also came to ask you something. I think it would be fun to have a little group of friends meeting here at The Coffee Cottage like the ladies do on Tuesday evenings? What do you think?"

Pam asked, "Do you have someone in mind to be your leader?"

Almost in unison Carson and Laney said, "Kaitlyn, we vote for you if you're willing."

Overwhelmed with emotion, Pam turned to Kaitlyn. "You are the perfect person. The girls love and look up to you so much. Will you?"

Kaitlyn nodded, realizing the responsibility entrusted to her. She would need to ask that same question – the one about Jesus being in the room – of herself and often. Consistently modeling a joyful spirit and integrity to these girls was vital to their walks with Jesus.

What about your own choices? Would you be embarrassed for Jesus to walk in while you're watching a certain TV show? What about the songs on the radio in the car, and He hops in the passenger seat? When choosing entertainment for yourself and your family, why not ask this question, and answer it honestly. Make the best decision to honor God in it all. Uprightness and integrity are easily lost, but not so easily regained.

NOTE: Carley! is a fictional singer/rock star. Any resemblance to any specific singer/rock star, other entertainer or person is coincidental and unintentional.

Cinnamon in Scripture

Modeling Integrity

Botanic Name: Cinnamomum verum; oil steam-distilled from the bark of the tree; native to China, East India, Ceylon (current day Sri Lanka), Malabar (Southwest coast of India)

Strength, stability, warmth, abundance – Jesus the Christ arrived in earthly flesh, bringing heavenly abundance and stability to lives and hearts trusting in the strength and warmth of His love. He came and made His home among us.

Cinnamon is the most beloved and easily recognized scent of the Christmas season. In **The Essence of Courage** we learned among the fruit of the Spirit cinnamon represents goodness.[62] In Hebrew context cinnamon's erect or upright rolls and sweetness suggest integrity and abundance. Can you taste and smell all those Christmas treats?

The ingredient list for the incense recipe given by God to Moses included cinnamon. Ancients used it to help preserve meat. The incense being used with every substitutionary sacrifice in the Old Testament helped to surround the altar with sweet aromas. The priests' garments, hair, and skin absorbed those scents. In this way, the men carried them home to their families. In Revelation we learn the prayers of the saints arise as incense to the throne of God where the real sacrifice, Jesus Christ, is seated with our Daddy God. The priests of old who offered the animal sacrifices as they awaited the coming Messiah found themselves steeped in the aromas of the incense. So does Jesus! Sacrifices were an everyday occurrence for the priests. Our prayers lifted to the throne room of God everyday, make upward drifting cinnamon a continuous experience for Jesus, our High Priest, too.

---

[62]Lynn U. Watson, *The Essence of Courage: Cultivating the Fruit of the Spirit in Solomon's Locked Garden and in Your Heart*, (Bartlett, Tennessee: Lynn U. Watson, 2016) Chapter 6, pages 111-128.

> *Therefore, He had to be like His brothers in every way, so that He could become a merciful and faithful high priest in service to God, to make propitiation for the sins of the people. For since He Himself was tested and has suffered, He is able to help those who are tested.*
>
> ~Hebrews 2:17-18

How good God is to send His only Son into the world as a little baby in a body of clay just like ours to live among us and love on us in real and tangible ways. God allowed Him to face every challenge we do and permitted the enemy every opportunity to tempt Him. Jesus maintained perfect uprightness. His abundant tenderness toward people provided a sweet balm.

No comparison exists to the goodness of our God. But His goodness in our lives overflows into a life of serving Him and others. God created us for the overflow – for the good works He prepared for us.

> *For we are His creation, created in Christ Jesus for good works, which God prepared ahead of time so that we should walk in them.*
>
> ~Ephesians 2:10

This next verse was spoken to a preacher, but it is such wise counsel when we are serious about this life we live in Christ.

> *And you yourself must be an example to them by doing good works of every kind. Let everything you do reflect the integrity and seriousness of your teaching.*
>
> ~Titus 2:7 (NLT)

A Woman of the Bible Experience the Joy of Integrity
Meet Elisheba, The First Pastor's Wife

Joy is strength.[63]
~Mother Teresa

When Moses by God's direction announced Aaron and his sons as the first priests, they carried the aromas of frankincense, myrrh, calamus, cassia, and cinnamon with them. Elisheba, Aaron's wife, welcomed him home, her own emotions affected by the new blend of aromas. She's the first pastor's wife whose life we find recorded in the Bible.

Had she witnessed the ceremony ordaining her husband? Did Aaron's new position come with expectations for her? What reactions came from her friends?

God had appointed Aaron spokesman for Moses when they stood before Pharaoh. Now God gave him responsibility for the sacrifices for the sins of the people. We know how people are. If an animal was blemished and refused by Aaron did the people quarrel or rise up against him? Did they remember the punishment God doled out when Aaron and Hur led the golden calf debacle and question why he gets this high station? Did they threaten his family, his wife?

The Bible remains especially quiet about Elisabeth. What we do know is found in a single verse.

> *Aaron married Elisheba. She was the daughter of Amminadab and the sister of Nahshon. She had Nadab, Abihu, Eleazar and Ithamar by Aaron.*
>
> ~Exodus 6:23

---

[63] Mother Teresa, quote found at https://www.christianquotes.info/images/mother-teresa-quote-joy/#axzz4srdh3loy (accessed 9/16/2017)

Elisheba's father and brother both served as Kings of the tribe of Judah. Marriage between descendants of Judah and Levi joined the kingly and priestly lineages, foreshadowing Jesus titles as King of Kings and our High Priest. Her name, the Hebrew form of Elizabeth, is defined as "God's oath" or "God is her oath." Born during a distressing time in the history of Israel, did her parents call on the hope of God's promises to Abraham? We realize in hindsight she was born near the end of the oppressive years in Egypt. That event remained in the unknowable future for her family.

So we know her name. For me, passages like this beg answers only available when we reach heaven. The daily test of her character — her uprightness and her kindness and her reactions — probably resemble those faced by pastor's wives ever since. Let's create a list of questions we might ask about Eliseba's particular circumstances. You may have more of your own to add. The answers remain open ended.

1. The people grumbled against Moses and Aaron. They complained about the food and the conditions once they crossed the Red Sea. Did the women come to Elisheba and Moses' wife letting them know they didn't believe their pastors had a clear picture. Maybe the women could talk some sense into them.
2. Aaron and Hur bowed to the people's request for another god. While the gold was being gathered, where was Elisheba? Did she stand at Aaron's side and encourage the foolishness? Had her women's intuition kicked in warning him to steer clear of this party?
3. We all know that a few determined individuals can create a grassroots movement difficult to stop. In fact, the few often stop at nothing to protect their desired outcome. Were the lives of Aaron and Elisheba's children threatened if he didn't build the calf? Did Elisheba buckle under the threats or does she find a way to stand back and still protect her family?

4. Two of Aaron and Elisheba's sons died because they failed to follow God's specific directions for offering holy fire. Anyone who has lost a child shares her pain. Did the people talk behind her back about how if she had been a better mother this wouldn't have happened? How did her grief affect her? How did it affect their marriage?

But Nadab and Abihu made an offering to the Lord by using fire that wasn't allowed. So they died.
~Numbers 26:61

5. Her sister-in-law, Miriam, was the women's ministry leader. Did they have a good relationship? Remember Aaron sided with Miriam against Moses. Was this another opportunity for Elisheba to offer Aaron Godly counsel that he ignored or did she encourage her husband to make a poor decision? The outcome of that encounter was ugly. Miriam contracted leprosy as a result.

As the cloud moved away from the tent, Miriam's skin suddenly became diseased, as white as snow. When Aaron turned toward her, he saw that she was diseased and said to Moses, "My lord, please don't hold against us this sin we have so foolishly committed. Please don't let her be like a dead baby whose flesh is half eaten away when he comes out of his mother's womb."

~Numbers 12:10-12

Either way, Aaron and Miriam repented and were restored. What part of any humiliation or embarrassment fell on Elisheba?

6. Trending stories of our day regularly criticize leadership on every level. People were people then no different than they are today. We may assume scrutinizing eyes followed every move of Elisheba's birth family. After marrying Aaron their

behavior as temple leader and his 'first-lady' was on prominent display for uninvited scrutiny. Did the people regularly serve minced-priest and his family at the Sabbath dinner table?

As His representatives, The Most High God expected integrity and abundant goodness of character from them. So did the people they served. Cinnamon's aroma surrounded them as a reminder of the importance of uprightness and sweet gentle spirits even in the face of criticism. God absolutely embodies those character traits – all the time. Humans do not. Humans include Aaron and Elisheba. Humans include the whole Israelite nation they served. Humans include you and me.

Elisheba and Aaron, similar to our church and civil leaders today, resided in an aquarium in full view of their admiring and not-so-admiring public. The complainers, of course, made certain their voices were heard like noisy gongs above all else. They may have been the minority, but they are the ones rattling snakes, creating vicious accusations without full information, reinterpreting the rules (The 10 Commandments + their own ideas), and encouraging others to play along. Remember that group of nomads — God's chosen people, but still nomads — demanded Aaron build the golden calf in the first place.

How did Eliseba handle critics of her husband and her family? Simply allowing her child to wear his hair the "wrong" way had the capability of creating a scandal. Was any one trustworthy of her confidence to discuss her own challenges or those of her family? Did she have true friends? Or did others befriend her to "be in the know" or to believe they found a more ideal position to have the priest's ear?

What significance can we place upon asking questions about a pastor's wife living between 1445 and 1406 B.C.?[64] We acknowledged people are still people. They have not changed through history. Pastor's families today face the same challenges Aaron and Eliseba's faced. What expectations do you have for your pastor and his family?

---

[64] http://biblehub.com/timeline/ (accessed 8/7/2017)

How do you treat them? Do you hold their lives up to examination under a microscope and excuse shortcomings in your own family?

Your garments and your world may or may not be perfumed with cinnamon and exotic spices, but God's expectations for His children are the same for all of us. Jesus, the one born to be our Most High Priest reminded us of this.

> *"It's easy to see a smudge on your neighbor's face and be oblivious to the ugly sneer on your own. Do you have the nerve to say, 'Let me wash your face for you,' when your own face is distorted by contempt? It's this I-know-better-than-you mentality again, playing a holier-than-thou part instead of just living your own part. Wipe that ugly sneer off your own face and you might be fit to offer a washcloth to your neighbor.*
>
> ~Luke 6:41-42 (The Message)

The Apostle Paul further encourages us to love and honor our leaders. Observe the overwhelming joy brought into their lives when we do. (HINT: Encourage each other in the very same way.)

> *And now, friends, we ask you to honor those leaders who work so hard for you, who have been given the responsibility of urging and guiding you along in your obedience. Overwhelm them with appreciation and love!*
>
> ~1 Thessalonians 5:13 (The Message)

We abundantly shower our pastors and ministry leaders with gifts during the Christmas season. Why not show them special appreciation and love for 'no particular reason' at random times throughout the year.

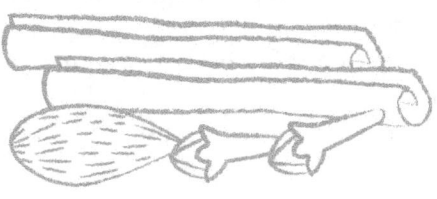

Cinnamon Essence Droplets

Don't run from tests and hardships, brothers and sisters. As difficult as they are, you will ultimately find joy in them; if you embrace them, your faith will blossom under pressure and teach you true patience as you endure.
~James 1:2 (VOICE)

Fun Facts:
- Cinnamon sticks are actually called cinnamon quills.[65]
- Sweet and Salty dishes may both be enhanced by cinnamon.[64]
- Cinnamon oil adds warm spicy notes to food, but destroys mosquito larvae.[66]
- National Cinnamon Crescent Roll Day is celebrated April 10.[67]
- Manganese, fiber, iron, and calcium are found in cinnamon. Each teaspoon of cinnamon contains 6 calories.[68]
- Cinnamon was one of the first traded spices. It was brought from Sri Lanka to Palestine.[67]
- Chinese documented use of cinnamon in 2800 B.C.[67]

---

[65] http://www.thatsitfruit.com/buzz/10-interesting-facts-about-cinnamon/, (accessed 9/16/2017)
[66] https://www.foodbeast.com/news/7-unique-facts-that-you-didnt-know-about-cinnamon/, (accessed 9/16/2017)
[67] https://mobile-cuisine.com/did-you-know/cinnamon-roll-fun-facts/, (accessed 9/16/2017)
[68] http://blog.americanspice.com/index.php/fun-cinnamon-facts-and-recipes/, (accessed 9/16/2017)

Your Turn:
- Cinnamon syrup may be made from three simple ingredients: cinnamon sticks, granulated sugar, and water. Tasty in beverages, on cereal, on pancakes, and more.[69]
- Cinnamon chips are tasty in cookies and breads especially during the holidays. Did you know you can make your own cinnamon chips?[70]
- Create a playlist of worship songs and hymns encouraging you to find abundant joy and strength in Jesus.
- To go along with our palm tree themed Christmas tree (see chapter on Palm), find a large shell dish. Fill it with paper pearls adorned with Scriptures about finding our joy and strength in the Lord. Decorate the shell with cinnamon sticks.

---

[69] http://www.theyummylife.com/Cinnamon_Simple_Syrup, (accessed 9/16/2017)

[70] http://afewshortcuts.com/homemade-cinnamon-baking-chips/, (accessed 9/16/2017)

Chapter 8

Citron
The Joy of Legacy

Cinnamon-Brosia and Friends Share About
Citron - The Joy of Legacy

Part 1

Diffusing Today: Lemon and Lime essential oils
Aromatic Influence: Helps to create a warm, invigorating, and lively atmosphere
Daily Delight: Italian Christmas Bread - Panettone
Musically: **We Three Kings**
Verse of the Day:
God's love is meteoric, his loyalty astronomic, His purpose titanic, his verdicts oceanic. Yet in his largeness nothing gets lost; Not a man, not a mouse, slips through the cracks.
~Psalm 36:5 (The Message)

October's "Fish and Beans" night delivered unexpected blessings. Mom and Dad's new life believing in Jesus surged. Overflow lavishly splattered on most everyone they encountered. Since Mom and I reconciled on Mother's Day, both of them found a new sense of urgency to take the monthly ministry Gramps had started to a whole new level. They embraced the very behavior that forty-seven years ago, drove them into a misguided lifestyle away from Jesus and away from family for far too long.

Present for every "Fish and Beans" night since May, Sandra and Andy — my mom and dad — initiated a plan for the October night to be one of remembrance and testimonies. They prepared to share their stories and invited others to do the same. At the September gathering Andy urged the others, "Invite young friends in our community, too – like the one's Gramps would have invited years ago." Tonight was the night. Old friends, new friends, neighbors, and soon-to-be friends packed the cottage. My heart swelled as my dad began.

"Five years ago my best friend chose to drive under the influence, an activity he considered 'no big deal at all.' For decades he 'smoked' or 'shot up' at least a couple times a week and drove under the influence. This particular night Jeff's irresponsibility resulted in a fiery crash that ended his life and the lives of a whole family - a mom, a dad, and three young children. What if that had been my own three children?

"Deeply grieved, I withdrew from life and stared at the ceiling far more hours than I care to remember. A quiet voice within beckoned me, 'Remember Ben's story.'

"Sandra's dad's behavior sent me on this life-long quest for anything but what he 'preached.' Now I should revisit his story? I laughed at the persistent shadow clambering at my side, but the day I sent that dark animal packing, realization dawned. Oh how parallel our stories stacked up.

"Sandra's dad and I both provided for our families, but snorted at living like they held importance in our lives. Instead we both honored the god of self. We indulged in our own little worlds and surrounded ourselves with friends who kept us there. We served long-term personally-created prison sentences. We both lost our best friend to foolish behavior. After his brother died in the boating accident, Ben sat on the porch staring beyond Miss Dot's garden while many sunsets came and went. In my grief, I visited the ceiling often. The cracks and peeling paint reminded me how badly I messed up and messed up my family. I evaluated my behavior as far worse than Ben's.

"Ben remained silent during the years his brother abused Sandra, allowing the damage to accumulate. I seethed over that for years, then abused my own children and allowed others inappropriate actions against them as well.

"Eventually understanding flashed my way. Sandra and I foolishly disbelieved the change in Ben's life. A theme of the day prevailed: 'Trust no one over thirty.' For those who paused in their young lives even a moment, Ben testified to what God had done in his own. A tiny handful listened. Not us. Ben's been gone sixteen years now. The opportunity to ask forgiveness or seek his wisdom departed with him. In desperation I ran to Miss Dot, knees wobblin' and heart pounding. Fear of rejection crushed me with the weight of a two and half ton pick-up.

"Instead of expected judgment, I still feel Gram's arms embracing me in the softest, yet strongest hug I've ever known. We visited the wounds from the past. We also opened Ben's Bible, safely kept for this anticipated day. Dated notes and prayers all through its pages told the story of his own pain and his hopes for his daughter and her family. Left speechless and with canyon-deep regret, I fell to my knees sobbing. Gram knelt beside me and led me to Jesus that day. She gifted me Gramp's Bible. I've added my prayers to his. I thank God for His amazing forgiveness for even me - the most messed up person I know. I thank him for restoring my relationship with my children and Gram. I pleaded for Him to provide a way to demonstrate to Sandra how much her dad loved her and her Daddy God did, too, and always will."

Sandra added her own story. Before they finished sharing, sniffling sound effects perpetrated by leaky eye sockets pricked the quietness. Staccato slaps of hands put together for God's glory followed. Andy encouraged others to share.

"There must be more amazing stories out there. When we position ourselves for vulnerability, our hurts, screw ups and God's faithfulness bring comfort and encouragement to others who may believe they're the only ones who feel that way.'"

Mandy stood by her seat. "When we said our good-byes to my grandmother a few years ago, family gathered at her bedside. Her condition deteriorated day by day. Her eyes closed now. Limited communication meant an occasional squeeze of her hand around ours. In a twinkling she opened her eyes, stared into the corner of the room and asked, 'Do you see it?'

"My cousin asked her, 'Is it scary?'

'No, it's beautiful. Everything is beautiful.'

"Taking her last breath, all of us knew she glimpsed heaven - she found peace and joy in the arms of Jesus. The lives of skeptics in our family changed in that moment. That day they chose to believe Jesus and His promises, and two of them invited Him into their lives."

Carol went next, remembering how alcohol had nearly destroyed her son's family. She praised God for changes evident in Justin's life. "Justin and his family relocated recently, and I'm so excited about the inner-city ministry he has begun. He's teaching young people how to repair and restore old bicycles. Their hard work gives them ownership in their 'new' transportation. It's an opportunity to gain their trust and share Jesus. Three young men dedicated their lives to Jesus last week. So much thankfulness and so much to look forward to."

Jane spoke up. "I've kept this hidden from all of you, because of embarrassment mostly – I guess. Having led the women's small group here at The Coffee Cottage for several years, I'm convicted – I haven't been totally honest with all of you. Maybe you would think less of me.

"Before Alex and I married and chose to raise our family here in Pearlville, my family belonged to a controlling church - more of a cult, really. A friend invited me to a gathering at her home, where a young man presented Jesus in a way I never experienced before. I decided at that moment this Jesus would be my new best friend. Those in the small group guarded my choice, because the worst of repercussions loomed when my family learned what I had done.

"The last few months of my senior year sped past like a bullet. I continued to attend the gatherings. My family's suspicions grew like the Pharisees peppermint crop. They confronted me the night of graduation — my secret, secret no longer.

"That night I lost my family and my home. Family cut me off. The attack hit worse than death. When the end came for my mom, no one even told me she died. I learned the sad news four years later.

"I experience sadness everyday over my losses, but no regrets for choosing Jesus! My friend's family took me in without hesitation. I saw them as Jesus in shoes. They loved on me when often I was most unlovable. They helped me back up. I learned from their example to love like Jesus loves and how to be a best friend to Him, too. Everyday since saying, "yes," to Jesus I encounter new and profound reasons to live in thankfulness and expectancy. My choice to follow Jesus never made my life easy - far from it. Still He remains the number one love of my life.

"You know that young man as Alex. My friend brought me along that night, but Alex is the first person who shared the hope of Jesus with me. Watching my new faith bloom in spite of the pain, he soon promised to walk by my side through the turmoil of my decision and whatever life tossed our way. He asked, and I said, "yes," yet again. We've done life together for forty years. While you never heard the story, you know his amazing example of loving like and living for Jesus."

More tears flooded the room. Holt picked up his guitar and quietly began to play *"Tell Your Heart to Breathe Again."* The song seemed to fit the moment where everyone found themselves —one of solemnity and one of joy. One of deep retrospect and promised celebration. (Allow yourself to be amazed by the story behind the song, too. Check it out at the links below.)

During the beauty of that moment, Ashley reached out to Carol. "We moved thirteen times in twelve years. This is so difficult to share, especially with a few classmates here tonight. Can we talk alone? I sense you are someone worthy of my trust."

Carol led Ashley away from the group and into the kitchen, protecting Ashley's confidence. Ashley spilled her story:

"With each move Dad promised a fresh start. No more drinking. Each time his new 'friends' quickly convinced him to join their partying at the bar. The arguments between him and mom boiled behind closed doors. Every one instilled more and more fear. Question I asked myself: We move so much, why make friends? The kids at school had no idea and didn't care. No one worth trusting exists. Mom allowed his behavior to destroy our lives.

"When we moved here to Pearlville three years ago, Mom finally found the courage to separate from him. My brother, Ryan, and I still had contact. We observed changes in his behavior, but chose to not believe the transformation. Every moment, every phone call, every text message alerted us to potential tragedy and sent my stomach tumbling. I've gone through high school so alone. I contemplated suicide more than once.

"Ryan suggested coming tonight. 'What?' I said. Listen to stories from a bunch of old people? Our family attended church regularly. Ryan volunteered to help cut grass and help with stuff around the church. He met Andy. Andy invited Ryan. Ryan convinced me to tag along.

"I'm glad we came. All of you sharing about lives really changed. For a year now Dad has coached young boys on the soccer field. He tells them stories of God at work in his life, encouraging them to make better choices. At least that's what he tells us about it. I laugh at his fake makeover, and I push him away again and again. He and mom got back together a few months ago. On guard, always waiting for the next bad time to come, my life resembles a rocky maze of land mines waiting for the misstep, detonating another explosion. Peace eludes me.

"Tonight gives me hope - hope for my dad, hope the pain of my childhood can be reconciled. Maybe one day my story will encourage others. I need help to sort it all out, but answers to my desperate prayers for friends walking by my side or at least someone to understand remained unanswered."

Carol slipped her arms around Ashley, and recounted more of her story of pain, anguish, and tears. Her son, Justin, had lived a life parallel to Ashley's dad. "Eventually Justin turned his life around, but not until he made many poor choices. He spent lots of money on liquor and emotionally abused his family. Driving under the influence led to hurting others, losing his license three times, and ultimately doing time behind bars." Carol promised Ashley her continued friendship. "Introduce me to your mom, too. I love how God uses our trials to create new opportunities to love on one another." The music stilled, and another voice spoke. "Let's rejoin the group," Ashley suggested.

Cinnamon-Brosia and Friends Share About
Citron – The Joy of Legacy

Part 2

The voice they heard from the kitchen belonged to Pastor Able. Three years ago he began as an assistant pastor, working with Pastor Gary.

"Raised in a Jewish home, fifteen years ago I came to know Yeshua (Jesus) as my Savior. This week the Jewish community celebrates the Feast of Tabernacles."

Pastor Able picked up a copy of the Bible kept at The Coffee Cottage. The Message version delivers straight-forward, easy-to-understand text. He turned to Leviticus and read:

> *"So, summing up: On the fifteenth day of the seventh month, after you have brought your crops in from your fields, celebrate the Feast of God for seven days. The first day is a complete rest and the eighth day is a complete rest. On the first day, pick the best fruit from the best trees; take fronds of palm trees and branches of leafy trees and from willows by the brook and celebrate in the presence of your God for seven days—yes, for seven full days celebrate it as a festival to God. Every year from now on, celebrate it in the seventh month. Live in booths for seven days—every son and daughter of Israel is to move into booths so that your descendants will know that I made the People of Israel live in booths when I brought them out of the land of Egypt. I am God, your God."*
> ~Leviticus 23:39-43 (The Message)

"As I studied the Jewish (Old Testament) Scriptures alongside the New Testament, details of the pieces fitting together amazed me. We could all celebrate these feasts. What God gave first to Moses, all foreshadowed the coming Messiah. I am bold to speak Truth, but I acknowledge not everyone's perspective reflects my own enthusiasm. I pray you'll hear my heart tonight and become excited with me.

"Pastor Gary and I often study the feasts together, marveling at their place in the Jesus story. It may be easy for a long-time Christian raised in the church to say, 'Sure that Old Testament prophecy is fulfilled by Jesus.' But digging deeper, the bigger picture shows us Jesus in the details of each of the Old Testament feasts in ways all too quickly passed by without notice.

"This week the Jewish people celebrate the Feast of Tabernacles, also known as Sukkot. It is an amazing time of remembrance of God's faithfulness and the legacies of His people to future generations. The expectant celebration of His continued love and leading in our lives comes to life in dance, song, and shared stories of His faithfulness. The branches and fruit found in God's instructions make up a festive prop called a lulav. By tradition, specific guidelines exist for handling and holding the citron portion of it. The citron, a bumpy lemon looking fruit, represents the Godly man or woman walking in relationship with Jesus. Their lives, full of fruit, provide seeds for future generations. Your stories shout the joy of remembrance and legacy, the joy of Sukkot — the Feast of Tabernacles!

"Cinnamah-Brosia, this current inspirational collection you're creating from your friends' stories features fruits and aromas of the holidays in anticipation of celebrating Christmas - Jesus birthday, right?"

I nodded in agreement, and Pastor Able continued. "In the Christmas story, the apostle John tells us, *'And the Word became flesh and dwelt among us.'* Literally translated that passage reads differently:

> *And the Word became flesh and tabernacled among us.*
> *We looked upon His glory, the glory of the one and only*
> *from the Father, full of grace and truth.*
> ~John 1:14 (TLV)

"Research on the subject suggests December 25 was chosen centuries ago to celebrate Jesus birthday, giving Christians a special day of their own coinciding with many of the pagan festivals. Another consideration is December 25th's proximity to Hannuakah, a celebration of dedication for the reconstruction of the temple.[72] Jesus participated in Hannuakah with His disciples.

> *Then came Hanukkah; it was winter in Jerusalem. Yeshua was walking in the Temple around Solomon's Colonnade. Then the Judean leaders surrounded Him, saying, "How long will You hold us in suspense? If You are the Messiah, tell us outright!"*
> ~John 10:22-24 (TLV)

"Either way, Church fathers hoped by placing the date of Jesus' birth close to one or more of these dates the real meaning of His nativity would become the season's focus.

"Many Biblical scholars believe Jesus' birth, though, occurred during the Feast of Tabernacles. Pastor Gary and I love looking at the research and putting the pieces together. It would be a privilege to share resources with you. I promise his gentile faith and my Messianic Jewish faith grow richer and we both fall deeper in love with Jesus with each new discovery."[73][74][75]

---

[72] http://www.thetransformedsoul.com/additional-studies/spiritual-life-studies/the-intertestamental-period-and-its-significance-upon-christianity (accessed 9/23/2017)
[73] https://youtu.be/KmwuTJG4yV0 (accessed 9/16/2017)
[74] https://youtu.be/iZ8WLRNEDWg (accessed 9/16/2017)
   http://www.jewishjewels.org/news-letters/sukkot/ (accessed 9/22/2017)

NOTE: A few resources are listed in the footnotes on the previous page to help you make your own discoveries about The Feast of Tabernacles and Jesus Nativity. You'll uncover many gems of truth and connection well beyond this one feast. Happy learning! Happy Sukkot! Happy Jesus' Nativity! How many years of His holy legacy is that to celebrate!

The Essence of Citron in Scripture
Recounting God's Faithfulness

Botanical name: Citrus medica;
essential oil old-pressed from the rind;
native to Southeast Asia

Today we connect citrons, God's Word, and Jesus nativity. How many recognize a citron when they see it? Are you puzzled? I was too. Then I learned its role as the mama citrus of all citrus we enjoy today — lemons, limes, oranges, tangerines, and more.

Look around at Christmas decorations and recipes. Lemons, a close relative of citron, abound! An orange falls from Alfonzo's Christmas stocking in Laura Ingalls Wilder's ***Farmer Boy***. Many of us remember the orange in the toe of our stockings, too. Traced back even further, St. Nicholas' bags of gold tossed through the window of the poor girls' home landed in their stockings. The hue of the coins gleamed as golden as citrus. Citrus of all varieties, along with cinnamon and clove, more than any other scents spark nostalgia and enthusiasm for the holiday season. Studies conclude this to be true in the fall and winter, while different ones dominate in spring and summer.[76]

God directed Moses in the celebration of special feasts. The grand finale of all the feasts arrives with Sukkot in late September or early October. This final feast of the Jewish calendar falls during the harvest ingathering. What perfect timing for remembrance of God's faithfulness and for giving thanks for the bounty He provides. Generosity, charitable deeds, and joyful celebrations with family, friends, and even strangers highlight the season.

God's specific instructions required four species of plant life necessary to celebrate. Three are spelled out: palm, myrtle, and willow. The fourth is "the fruit of the goodly tree." Some Bible

---

[76] http://io9.gizmodo.com/5717190/cinnamon-is-scientifically-proven-to-be-the-most-christmas-y-smell-in-the-world (accessed 9/16/2017)

versions name the citron. No citron trees grew in the Middle East at the time the directives were given. A great likelihood exists, olive was the fruit. However, as people we create traditions. Around 200 B.C. citron was introduced in Israel. It became the fruit of choice used for the celebration then, and in Jesus day. It continues to be the fruit of choice in celebration of Sukkot/Feast of Tabernacles by the Jewish people today.

For everything this feast embodied, joy ruled! Ezra read to the people following the rebuilding of the temple. The people mourned since the time of Joshua, no one celebrated the Feast of Tabernacles. Ezra reminded them of new beginnings:

> *Go back to your homes, and prepare a feast. Bring out the best food and drink you have, and welcome all to your table, especially those who have nothing. This day is special. It is sacred to our Lord. Do not grieve over your past mistakes. Let the Eternal's own joy be your protection!*
>
> ~Nehemiah 8:10 (VOICE)

To celebrate according to the Father's instructions necessitates gathering the four species including the fruit of the goodly tree. This fruit today is definitely citron, and it is big business in autumn. The citron portion is referred to as the "etrog."

> "The etrog is said to symbolize the heart. The sages say the word "etrog" is an acronym (Hebrew alphabet) for "faith…, repentance…., healing…, and redemption…" Also, the initials of the words "Let not the foot of pride overtake me" (Psalm 36:12) - spell the word "etrog," suggesting that the fruit of the humble heart is most beautiful in the eyes of heaven…"[77]

---

[77] http://www.hebrew4christians.com/Holidays/Fall_Holidays/Sukkot/sukkot.html (accessed 7/20/2017)

The heart of the righteous is filled with the joy of the Lord, rejoices in gratitude for blessings received, spreads a joyful bounty bestowing gifts and sharing the Good News of Jesus!

Hybridizations of Citrus medica produced every variety of citrus we know today. Referring back to Pastor Able's message at Fish and Beans night for Citron, we discovered the belief of many scholars that Jesus birth took place during this feast. If so, it comes during the season our keen sense of smell reminds us of the joyful season we are celebrating: Thanksgiving, Christmas, Sukkot/Feast of Tabernacles. Maybe the story of citrus as part of Christmas goes back to Laura Ingall Wilder's story or even further to St. Nicholas. Or perhaps we attribute it to this festival of great joy (and the citron) first celebrated by Moses and the children of Israel. What a long legacy of remembrance, celebration, and JOY!

Let those who fear the Lord say,
"His faithful love endures forever."
~Psalm 118:4

Whenever you see lemons used in decorations of the season, remind yourself of the joy of remembrance. Recount with exuberant celebration God's faithfulness in your life.

A Woman of the Bible Experiences the Joy of Legacy
This Time Leah Praised the Lord

*Take the stones that failure throws at you
and build legacies the world will always remember you for.*[78]
~ Israelmore Ayivor, *Become a Better You*

Lack of integrity on the part of her father positioned Leah as the unwanted wife. The truth remained hidden throughout the ceremony and during activities in the bridal chamber. Awakening to a husband incensed by her father's manipulation transformed her dreamy wedding night to a marital nightmare. Jacob didn't want Leah. He didn't love Leah. He loved Rachel — oh how he loved Rachel. Willingness to work seven more years to claim her for himself spoke volumes of scorn to Leah. She would give Jacob children, but he would never give her his love.

Jealous for sure, would she also come to hate her younger sister? Indifference found no home here, one wife consistently chosen, loved, and favored over the other. Leah set out to earn Jacob's love, giving him sons — so important to the family legacy. Neither Reuben, Simeon, nor Levi turned Jacob's heart toward her in spite of Rachel's barrenness. With the birth of her fourth son, Leah chose to praise God perhaps abandoning all hope of winning more than a few bedroom encounters with her husband.

She named this son Judah. At this point Leah stopped having children. A contest ensued between the sisters, giving their maids to Jacob to produce further offspring. Is Jacob loving this party, or what?! Leah bore him two more sons and a daughter. Eventually, two sons were born to Jacob through Rachel, only for him to lose her in childbirth with the second. With four different women Jacob fathered twelve sons and a daughter.

Leah said it well when she bore Judah:

---

[78] https://www.goodreads.com/author/show/7023141.Israelmore_Ayivor (accesed 9/22/2017)

> *"This time I will praise the Lord."*
> ~Genesis 29:35

She sang and worshipped an amazing God who missed none of the pain she bore. He twirled the whole situation around to create a legacy neither Leah nor Jacob even glimpsed much less imagined. Born to Rachel, Joseph was Jacob's favorite son. Through another disparaging story of duplicity and envy among siblings, his brothers sold him out to a doomed life as a slave. Or so they believed. God handed Joseph a key role in the deliverance of his family many years later. From Leah's son, Judah, however, came the Savior of the World. Through his line Jesus would be born. Great joy born, not for a moment, but for an eternity!

> *Then one of the elders tells me, "Stop weeping! Behold, the Lion of the tribe of Judah, the Root of David, has triumphed— He is worthy to open the scroll and its seven seals."*
> ~Revelations 5:5 (TLV)

As if that were not enough vindication for all she endured, through Leah's third son, Levi, came the priestly line - yet another set of very special players in the Jesus story. Responsibility for the sacrifices and all parts of the tabernacle and temple resided with the men of this lineage. The sacrifices they offered foreshadowed the nativity of Jesus and His ultimate sacrifice for our sin. Covered. Signed. Sealed. Delivered - with His victorious resurrection that followed on the first Easter morning.

The joy-filled legacy of God's love traveled to us through the faithfulness of the unloved wife! Sadly, she never knew the part she played in the nativity story during her time on earth. When you believe your life or that of a loved one has been flipped upside down and inside out, counting for little of value, God's economy reimagines and transforms the most unsightly situations into beautiful forevers. What stories from your life or that of your family and friends come to mind? We would be honored for you to share. We would be equally honored to pray for your upside down situations — God desires to shape them into a joyful tomorrow.[79]

---

[79] Our social media and email contact information may be found at the end of the book.

Citron Essence Droplets

Hallelujah!
Happy is the man who fears the LORD,
taking great delight in His commands.
His descendants will be powerful in the land;
the generation of the upright will be blessed.
Wealth and riches are in his house,
and his righteousness endures forever.
~Psalm 112:1-3

Fun Facts:

- Citron along with mandarin, pomelo, and papedas, are the four original citrus species from which all other citrus has been hybridized.[80]
- The citron tree bears fruit year round. As some ripen, more fruit appears.[78]
- As part of the lulav, citron represents the heart and also the person whose life evidences both good deeds and knowledge of Scripture. [81]
- In Hebrew the word for etrog/citron is "beautiful."[82]
- The etrog/citron tree requires much more water than most trees.[80]
- The pitam or flower of the citron must remain on the citron for it to be used for the festival of sukkot.[83]

---

[80] https://en.m.wikipedia.org/wiki/Citron (accessed 6/23/2017)
[81] http://www.jewfaq.org/m/etrog.htm (accessed 9/22/2017)
[82] http://www.chabad.org/holidays/JewishNewYear/template_cdo/aid/746603/jewish/Why-cant-I-use-a-lemon.htm (accessed 9/22/2017)
[83] http://www.specialtyproduce.com/produce/Etrog_Citron_8713.php (accessed 9/22/2017)

Your Turn:

- After Sukkot the peel of the citron is often candied as a treat. If available in a market near you (most likely to find in October in Northern Hemisphere), find a recipe for candied citron and create a batch for your family or as a gift.
- Learn more about Sukkot (Feast of Tabernacles). Gather the four species of the lulav (this includes citron) and create your own holiday prop.
- YouTube and similar sites host numerous videos and music videos featuring the lulav. Search for and view a few of these, and experience the joy and celebration!
- Candied fruits such as citron are often used in baking Christmas breads and cookies. Find a recipe and create a batch for your family.
- Add prayers for your family to your Bible like Gramps did, creating a beautiful legacy for the next generation.[84]

---

[84] https://entrustedministries.com/blog/the-legacy-of-the-well-loved-word (accessed 9/7/2017)

Chapter 9

Palm
The Joy of Celebration

Cinnamah-Brosia and Friends Share About
Palm – The Joy of Celebration

Diffusing Today: Eucalyptus Blue and Lemon Essential Oils
Aromatic Influence: Helping to create, enhance, and invigorate a joyful space
Daily Delight: Date Nut Bread
Musically: ***Joy to the World***
Verse of the Day:

> *The news of Your rich goodness is no secret—*
> *Your people love to recall it and*
> *sing songs of joy to celebrate Your righteousness.*
> Psalm 145:7 (VOICE)

"The service morphed suddenly into grand celebration — the palm waving variety — the one that has teary-eyed worshippers rejoicing with the angels in heaven. Star's husband, Tom, baptized their daughter, Jessica, that beautiful morning." Cinnamah-Brosia paused in the middle of chatting with the Tuesday night group. "Star, you tell the story!"

C-B and her friend, Star, lead a group of at-risk teen girls, but Star rarely accepts C-B's invites to join the Tuesday night group. Tonight she agreed to pop in and share her testimony of God's faithfulness in her family's life. She began….

"Thank you for your hospitality. All of you are aware my faith has been deeply challenged the last several years. In the midst of my pain, our daughter Jessica's rebellion demanded attention, over-the-top discipline, and interventions. She made the term strong-willed-child look silly. She experimented with alcohol in junior high, moving on to serious drugs in high school.

"Teachers observed the same potential in her my husband and I believed she possessed. The demons of addiction claiming large amounts of real estate in her mind and her heart held her hostage.

My mom and my twin brother, her Uncle Shane, penetrated the fog occasionally. Jessica's intentions to change, however, always proved minimal and short-lived.

"Her living arrangements bordered on third world. Smart, but lacking skills and education coupled with the addictions, prevented her ability to work regularly and care for herself. She moved in with an equally unmotivated boyfriend. Baby Grace arrived premature and addicted. Tom and I welcomed Grace into our home, loved her, met all her needs, and, of course, introduced her to Jesus. Grace grew and blossomed. This contented ten-year-old prays for her mom everyday. Jessica continued on the weary path to nowhere.

"Her Uncle Shane died in a motorcycle accident a year and a half ago. My mom passed a few weeks later. Cinnamon-Brosia watched me spiral into the pit of despair. We led the Bible study for those at-risk girls. I wondered who I was fooling. My own daughter disregarded my counsel. I almost quit right before the party. C-B and I planned a princess party for the girls. The date we set landed just a month after the unexpected loss of my brother and mom. Well, C-B planned the party, really. I reluctantly tagged along, dejected and sitting quietly in the corner. Instead of complaining about my less than helpful attitude, God allowed C-B to include me. Her loving care toward me began restoring my faith.

"The tragic losses forced me face down covered in scrapes and bruises, but the deaths awakened a different Spirit in Jessica. First she asked for Granny's Bible. Shocked, but thrilled by the request, I immediately handed her the well-worn book. I knew Mom's prayers for her trailed all through its pages.

"A few months passed. Jessica visited regularly. Young as she is, Grace realized something different happening in her mother's life. For years Grace feared seeing her mom. Now she looks forward to her visits. My dad, admittedly very lonely, hardly contained himself. Not usually an emotional man, he chose to embrace her fully in his time of need — and hers. Jessica transitioned from the unsavory living conditions and made her new home with Granddad! Emotions from pain of the losses and joy for Jessica's new-found faith played out like a yo-yo. Doubtful any energy for the challenges remained in me, I'm so grateful Dad found a new purpose for his own life as he walked her through hills and valleys she encountered creating a different life.

"Jessica asked to help C-B and me at the Bible studies. While still too embarrassed by her past to make a public commitment to Jesus, we saw a light gleaming in answer to our prayers. She learned more about Him alongside the girls we served.

"Just before close of service Sunday our pastor announced Jessica's baptism. Those who knew the trials we endured surrounded the baptistery — a cloud of witnesses with leaky eyes and smiles as big as heaven joining our celebration of great joy — a glimpse of a palm-waving party around the crystal sea!"

NOTE: In Lynn's family while she was growing up, Date Nut Bread made an appearance at every festive celebration. Date palms have dotted the Judean landscape for thousands of years. In this section we're looking at palms symbolic of celebration in Scripture. Lynn shared the recipe with us. Slices of this rich moist bread slathered with real butter are a favorite at The Coffee Cottage. She's given us permission to share the recipe with you, too. Visit http://lynnuwatson.com/date-nut-bread-recipe-gone-awol-hidden-under-our-noses/ to discover a funny story about the recipe.

The only reference Lynn has for this recipe is a copy in her mom's recipe collection. Any similarity to any recipe found elsewhere is unintentional and by coincidence.

Grace's Date Nut Bread

For the date mixture you'll need:
2 ½ cups pitted dates
2 cups hot water*
2 tsp baking soda
Mix these three ingredients together. Set aside, and allow to cool.

For the batter you'll need:
2 cups sugar*
2 eggs
½ tsp salt
2 Tbls butter
1 tsp Vanilla
4 cups flour
1 cup chopped pecans

Cream sugar and eggs together with an electric mixer. Mix in salt, butter, and vanilla. Fold in the flour and the date mixture alternately. (Add about 1 cup of flour followed by ¼ of the date mixture each time.) Continue in this matter until all of the flour and date mixture has been added. Stir in nuts. Pour into five 5 well-greased mini-loaf pans.
Bake 20-25 minutes at 350 degrees.
Bread is done when toothpick inserted in top of loaf comes out clean, or when internal temperature (measured with a meat thermometer) reaches 185 degrees.

* * *

*One (1) cup honey may be substituted for the two (2) cups sugar in this recipe.
If you use the honey, reduce the amount of water to 1¾ cups

The Essence of Palm in Scripture

You're Invited to the Ultimate Beach Party

Botanical name: Phoenix dactylifera;
produces dates; oil is made from the kernel and the
fleshy part of the fruit; the leaves of the deciduous tree
are used for fuel and building material;
native to Assyria (current day Iraq)

Lying on a sunny beach with palm tree fronds dancing in the breeze paints a picture of happy times with family and friends – perhaps celebrating a special occasion — even Christmas. One holiday season my husband and I ventured out for a week on a Caribbean cruise. Now you know there were palms everywhere in those paradise-like islands. And, yep, in celebration of the season islanders decorated the palm trees in miles of strings of lights. Palms wave their regal branches in celebration all through the pages of Scripture, too. Let's look in on three of those times.

The same party introducing us to citron included palm branches. We've arrived at the last essence of this inspirational collection. We learned God's command to continuously celebrate this festival throughout all generations. In these verses God instructed Moses in the celebration of the Festival of Tabernacles:

> *"You are to celebrate the Lord's festival on the fifteenth day of the seventh month for seven days after you have gathered the produce of the land. There will be complete rest on the first day and complete rest on the eighth day. On the first day you are to take the product of majestic trees—palm fronds, boughs of leafy trees, and willows of the brook—and rejoice before the Lord your God for seven days. You are to celebrate it as a festival to the Lord seven days each year.*

> *This is a permanent statute for you throughout your generations;*
>
> ~Leviticus 23:39-41a

Moving into the New Testament, nearing the outskirts of Jerusalem we hear the hosannas and take in the spectacle of the crowds waving palm branches in celebration of Jesus, the King of Kings — a red-carpet welcome provided by green palms instead.

> *The next day, when the large crowd that had come to the festival heard that Jesus was coming to Jerusalem, they took palm branches and went out to meet Him. They kept shouting: "Hosanna! He who comes in the name of the Lord is the blessed One—the King of Israel!"*
>
> ~John 12:12-13

John, the same man who penned this account of the first Palm Sunday, received the vision of Revelation – of the heavenly celebration to come. Once again palms line the imagery.

> *After I heard about these who would be sealed, I looked and saw a huge crowd of people, which no one could even begin to count, representing every nation and tribe, people and language, standing before the throne and before the Lamb, wearing white robes and waving palm branches. They cried out with one loud voice.*
>
> **Crowd:** *Salvation comes only from our God, who sits upon the throne, and from the Lamb.*
>
> ~Revelation 7:9-11 (VOICE)

Palm branches span the history of God's people from the Torah though the Gospels and into the Revelation of eternity awaiting Jesus return. An up-close view of each celebration, reveals interesting facts.

Palms are one of the four items of the lulav of the Feast of Tabernacles. Within the instructions to Moses for this celebration, God included the building of sukkats or booths – temporary shelters, also known as tabernacles.

Let's revisit God's Word in the Gospel of John, from the Tree of Life version:

> *And the Word became flesh and tabernacled among us. We looked upon His glory, the glory of the one and only from the Father, full of grace and truth.*
> ~John 1:14 (TLV)

Consider the possibility Jesus' birth occurred during the festival. Everyone came to Jerusalem to celebrate the Feast of Tabernacles. Bethlehem being close to Jerusalem, hosted many visitors. The stable where Jesus entered humanity resembles a temporary shelter. Many visitors overflowing the capacity of the little town of Bethlehem may have found it necessary to build their sukkah there. Jewish law required them to do that anyway. Haven't you always wondered where all the people stayed that there was no room for Mary and Joseph in this tiny town, but there was for everyone else? While the stable where they stayed may have been a more permanent structure than a sukkah, it may have served the dual purpose, offering a little extra protection for Mom and Baby. The next question is, did the shepherds build tabernacles in the fields? If so, from what were they constructed?

No oceans surrounded the land where the Israelites received God's instructions for celebrating the Feast of Tabernacles in the Promised Land. No tides rolled in before Jesus' birth. However, palm trees grew in the hot arid climate. From the website, *My Jewish Learning*, we learn of the laws for building the temporary structure.

> *Enough boughs should be placed upon the sukkah so as to have more shade than sun. If it has more sun than shade, it is invalid. It is therefore necessary to put on enough branches, so that even if they should dry up, there would still be more shade than sun*
> (Code of Jewish Law, Condensed Version, Chapter 134)[86]

A thick layer of palms easily provides the protection required. So common in the area, I envision shepherds waving them all the way back to the fields while shouting and sharing the Good News. He was born to be the King of Kings. The palms of celebration follow Jesus story from foreshadowing in the first days of the Promised Land to His first century (Christian Era) birth. Thirty-three years later, riding into Jerusalem the palm party gathered before Him, and the crowd hailed Him as King.

Revelation tells us God the Father hosts the ultimate party around the Crystal Sea. (Remember God created those island nations where palm trees wear the festive lights of the Christmas season. Do you think God loves the beach as much as most of us do?) All the people from the desert and the coast, cold climates and warm, wave those palm branches. God extends you a personal invitation to His beach party to wave your palm branches and worship Jesus with total abandon.

> *"Every person the Father gives me eventually comes running to me. And once that person is with me, I hold on and don't let go. I came down from heaven not to follow my own whim but to accomplish the will of the One who sent me. This, in a nutshell, is that will: that everything handed over to me by the Father be completed—not a single detail missed—and at the wrap-up of time I have everything and everyone put together, upright and whole. This is what my Father*

---

[86] http://www.myjewishlearning.com/article/laws-for-building-a-sukkah/ (accessed 9/16/2017)

wants: that anyone who sees the Son and trusts who he is and what he does and then aligns with him will enter real life, eternal life. My part is to put them on their feet alive and whole at the completion of time."

~John 6:37-40 (The Message)

Alive and whole and dancing with those palms around the crystal sea! Are you running to Jesus, trusting who He is and what He does? Align your life with His. The Beach Party awaits! I'll meet you there! It will be the best celebration of Jesus ever and forever!!!

A Woman of the Bible Who Experiences the Joy of Celebration
I Found My Coins: Let's Party

Each day holds a surprise. But only if we expect it can we see, hear, or feel it when it comes to us. Let's not be afraid to receive each day's surprise, whether it comes to us as sorrow or as joy it will open a new place in our hearts, a place where we can welcome new friends and celebrate more fully our shared humanity.[87]
~Henri Nouwen

My friend exuded joy when I suggested the woman who found her lost coin represents celebration for this section on palms. Here's why. She bubbled telling her story from a few days earlier. She had absent-mindedly left her phone on a park bench. "You know, I took my purse and my keys and just left my phone laying there. We were half-way home before I noticed. The sinking feeling hit me. No use turning around. I felt sure someone had claimed it by now. My husband asked his phone to call mine. His 'intelligent electronic assistant' did her job. A friendly voice answered the call. We made plans to be reunited with my 'whole life' because you know our phones hold that life hostage when they go missing. The couple, who found it, recently entrusted their lives to Jesus. We not only recovered my phone, but we witnessed their joy in their new-found faith. We all hugged in celebration that God knew and worked it all out perfectly. Waving palm branches would have been most appropriate."

We know little of the woman who lost her coin. She was a wife. As was often the case in her era, did the coins represent security to her in case of widowhood, adorn a scarf or headdress, or both?[88]

---

[87] Henri Nouwen, Quote found at: https://www.brainyquote.com/quotes/quotes/h/henrinouwe588384.html (accessed 9/22/2017)
[88] https://www.ucg.org/the-good-news/lessons-from-the-parables-the-parable-of-the-lost-coin-seeking-lost-people (accessed 9/7/2017)

We do know she lost a coin in her home. To spend much time sweeping and cleaning until she found it, she valued it highly — like a smart phone. Eureka! She found the coin, and invited her friends and neighbors to a joyful celebration! Her whole story occupies three verses of Scripture:

> *Or imagine a woman who has silver coins. She loses one. Doesn't she light a lamp, sweep the whole house, and search diligently until that coin is found? And when she finds it, doesn't she invite her friends and neighbors and say, "Celebrate with me! I've found that silver coin that I lost"? Can't you understand? There is joy in the presence of all God's messengers over even one sinner who changes his way of life.*
>
> ~~ Luke 15:8-10 (VOICE)

For both women, the incidents looked a lot like Christmas. Angels in heaven rejoice when a lost soul repents and discovers the Best Gift of all — Jesus – those angels celebrate like it is Christmas or Sukkot!

Any day is the perfect day to lead your friend to share your joy in Jesus. They all look a lot like Christmas or Sukkot (God with us - tabernacling among us) when a fellow human being welcomes Jesus into their heart. He entered our world the first time as a tiny infant. We await His triumphant return in the skies to escort us to heaven. He and the Father have prepared an unimaginable feast. They anticipate our arrival. Let's hurry on our way, and bring friends.

Palm Essence Droplets

*. . . while the morning stars sang together
and all the sons of God shouted for joy?*
~Job 38:7

Fun Facts:

- Palm trees are an important part of the eco-system and micro-environment of an oasis.[89]
- All parts of the palm tree are purposed for a wide variety of construction and manufacturing needs. Interestingly, these include dye, paper, surfboards, and wax.[86]
- In games and war, ancient Rome presented palms as symbols of victory.[90]
- The large seeds of the coco de mer variety of palm tree can be up to 20" diameter and weigh 66 pounds.[87]
- Valued for its importance for food and myriad other needs, the date palm tree is referred to as "the tree of life" in the Middle East. It also holds the honor of national symbol for Saudi Arabia and Israel.[91]
- One hundred days of 100 degree temps and plentiful water are required for the date palm to produce the very best fruit.[88]
- The seeds of the dates from the palm tree may be processed into a healthy coffee alternative.[92]

---

[89] https://datecoop.com/date-palm-trees-interesting-facts/ (accessed 6/23/2017)

[90] https://www.mnn.com/eart-matters/wilderness-resources/stories/10-surprising-facts-about-palm-trees (accessed 6/23/2017)

[91] https://www.mindbodygreen.com/0-18134/20-cool-facts-you-didn't-know-about-dates.html (accessed 6/23/2017)

[92] https://www.dateseedcoffee.com/blogs/coffee-substitutes-blog/86007300-date-palm-tree-interesting-facts (accessed 6/23/2017)

Your Turn:

- Gather some palm fronds (maybe on vacation) and weave them into a basket. A video demonstrating the process is found in the link below.[93]
- As we saw, palm branches in the Bible were used in celebrations. A quick search on Pinterest reveals numerous ideas for palm tree themed parties! Carry the theme through your next event!
- Consider using a palm tree as a Christmas tree. (Those living in areas where they readily grow are familiar with this idea.) The internet is full of ideas for lighting and decorating them.
- Make palm tree Christmas cookies. Cookie cutters for this activity are available from kitchen stores and online sources.
- Find (or freehand) a pattern for palm fronds. (Or you could trace you or your child's hand to use as palms.) Cut a trunk of brown paper or other material and the palm fronds from green. Write bible verses about joy and celebration on the fronds. Make a wreath with them welcoming guests to your home.

---

[93] https://youtu.be/EzUCugyQf8k (accessed 9/16/2017)

Before You Go...

A Few Parting Thoughts . . .

For four hundred years various empires ruled the dispersed nation of Israel. There was little peace, and there was no word from God. After Malachi, no other prophet had spoken. During this period lines were blurred between religion and politics, pagan cultures influenced the Jewish people, divisions arose among them, and confusion was more the rule than the exception.

Through most of those years the Jewish people were allowed to celebrate the feasts God had commanded. Spices and essential oils necessary to continue the rituals that had been laid out to Moses were available. Caravans along the spice routes still carried aromatic scents and seasonings. Mary would have known their many uses. When packing for the trip to Bethlehem she would have included them with her family's "camping food," her personal toiletries, and even in the layette for her baby.

Many of the scents, spices, and fruits scattered throughout the Bible have become treasured holiday aromas today. With the exception of the kings arrival with frankincense and myrrh, knowing which ones may have been present at Jesus' nativity would be speculation. By learning the spiritual connectedness of those mentioned in the Bible we realize new insights into the world Jesus entered.

I pray for your Christmas/Sukkot holidays to be enriched by the Baby whose nativity breaks those long years of waiting. God had once again spoken. Shepherds saw a great light in the heavens, and angels announced His birth. A man named Simeon studied the Scriptures well, was filled with the Holy Spirit, and believed God promised Him the opportunity to see salvation before he died. Old Testament law required Mary and Joseph to present Jesus at the temple along with a holy offering. When Mary and Joseph arrived at the temple in Jerusalem with Jesus. Simeon was present, he recognized the Light of the World, and he praised God!

God, you can now release your servant;
release me in peace as you promised.
With my own eyes I've seen your salvation;
it's now out in the open for everyone to see:
A God-revealing light to the non-Jewish nations,
and of glory for your people Israel.
~Luke 2:29-32 (The Message)

If you loved this inspirational collection,
thank you for leaving a review.

We love to hear from you, our readers:
- Sign up for our email list at http://LynnUWatson.com -- we will send you a FREE GIFT when you do.
- Visit our blog: http://LynnUWatson.com/blog We welcome your comments.
- Follow us on Facebook (leave comments and share, too, please) http://www.facebook.com/lynnuwatsonwriter
- And we are on Pinterest. http://http://www.pinterest.com/lynnuwatson
- Recipes featured at Cinnmah-Brosia's Coffee Cottage and gifts available in her gift shop are found on the website: http://LynnUWatson.com.
- In need of a website of your own. Thank you for considering http://http://www.watsondesign.us.
- Follow our cover artist, Allisha Mokry, on her blog: http://artfulexplorations.

Coming in 2018

Cinnamah-Brosia's Inspirational Collection for Women:
Volume 3

The Essence of Love

Cinnamah-Brosia's Profile

Birth Name: Cinnamon Amber Porter
Current Name: Cinnamon Amber (Porter) Fields
Nickname: Cinnamah-Brosia
Aliases: C-B, Cinnabro, Ms Cimmaba, Cinna-B, and many others her friends create
Birthday: May 14, 1970
Place of Birth: Pearlville, Missouri
Gender: Female
Eye Color: Green
Hair Color: Dark brown with rich red highlights
Height: 5'5"

Mother: Sandra Marie (Madison) Porter   1953
Father: Andrew (Andy) Robert Porter   1951
Siblings: Blossom Heather (Porter) Griffin   1971
   Stone Andrew Porter   1975
Maternal Grandmother: Dorothy Elizabeth (Perkins) Madison – a.k.a. Miss Dot) 1929-2016
Maternal Grandfather: Benjamin Henry Madison (Ben)   1926-2001
Education: Registered Nurse; completed nursing school May 1990
Husband: Jeremy Thomas Fields June 12, 1967
Wedding Date: May 12, 1990
Children: Kaitlyn Dorothy Fields, born November 10, 1994
     Aaron Thomas Fields, born May 22, 1995
     Caryn Joy Fields, bornNovember 24, 1999

Transportation: "Ruby," her bright red cruiser bicycle
Hobbies: aromatherapy, gardening, biking, all kinds of crafts (she rarely finds time for), reading, baking, entertaining, making others smile, and she's dreaming of others she hasn't shared yet.

Miss Dot's Café opened in 1966. After her passing in early 2016, Miss Dot's will provided funding specifically to renovate the cottage. Her grandmother and Kaitlyn envisioned the changes, and Cinnamah-Brosia promised Gram they would happen. The café would maintain its neighborly role in the community. A women's small group, formed several years earlier, continued to meet at the cottage during the construction phase. Although sometimes a challenge, they loved every minute of being part of, what they considered, community history in the making. In October 2016, Miss Dot's Café officially reopened as Cinnamah-Brosia's Coffee Cottage and Gift Shop.

Sophia's Corner: A stone fireplace as the backdrop, the corner is furnished with a gingerbread leather sofa and other comfy seating. The women's group meets here. It's rearranged a bit to be the "stage" area for musicians on Saturday nights when it opens as Fish and Beans Coffee House at the cottage. Sophia means wisdom in Greek, but it became known by that name in honor of the calico cat hanging around Miss Dot's Café. Gram called her Sophia, because she was wise enough to know where she would be loved and fed.

Fish and Beans Coffee House: In the early 1970's, Gram and Gramps opened Miss Dot's Café on Saturday evenings as a coffee house hangout for teens. Local musicians led those who attended in Jesus movement songs popular at the time. Coffee, of course, is made from beans, and fish made the name because of its symbolic connection to Christianity. Cinnamah-Brosia and friends revived the tradition at the coffee cottage.

Sign displayed above the coffee cottage's menu board:
Let all those you encounter leave happier
and better than they were before:
Have gentleness in your eyes – loving-kindness in your smile.
~~Unknown

Cinnamah-Brosia's friends – in the order you meet them in *The Essence of Joy*:

Haley – married to Dan – In *The Essence of Courage* the couple had a whole string of setbacks that had Haley questioning God. In *The Essence of Joy* she has just had an amazing encounter with Jesus.

Dan – Haley's husband (see above) – In *The Essence of Joy*, he is an amazing help at home while Haley is on a business trip.

Kaitlyn – Cinnamah-Brosia and Jeremy's oldest daughter – In *The Essence of Courge* she plans the renovation of Miss Dot's Café into Cinnamah-Brosia's Coffee Cottage. In *The Essence of Joy* she is recently engaged to Trevor. She and her friends plans to shop for bridesmaids' dresses is interrupted when Trevor is involved in an automobile accident.

Trevor – Kaitlyn's fiancé – Has an interesting experience and is sparred injury in an automobile accident.

Trevor's Mom & Dad – You meet them at the hospital following the accident.

Brooke – Kaitlyn's best friend

Stan – Trevor's boss

Sandra Porter – Cinnamah-Brosia's mom – In *The Essence of Courage* she was absent from Cinnamah-Brosia's life, and had inflicted much pain in the lives of her children. In *The Essence of Joy* her life has invited Jesus into her life, she has many regrets, and has come to ask for Cinnamah-Brosia's forgiveness. She hopes for a new start to their broken relationship.

Andy Porter – Cinnamah-Brosia's dad – In *The Essence of Courage* he was more involved in his children's childhood, but abused them and drove a wedge into their relationship. When we meet him again in *The Essence of Joy* we learn he made amends with the family and invited Jesus into his life two years ago. He has the opportunity to introduce his wife to Jesus, too. She had been very resistant to the changes in his life.

Gram – also known as Miss Dot. This is Sandra Porter's mom and Cinnamah-Brosia's grandmother. She passed away over a year and a half ago, but reminders of this Godly lady will be found all through the book, just as they were in *The Essence of Courage*.

Uncle John – Brother of Cinnamah-Brosia's grandfather. In *The Essence of Coruage* he was mentioned without name. He died many years ago in a boating accident.

Gramps – also known as Ben. Cinnamah-Brosia's grandfather. He also is deceased, but memories of him are scattered throughout both books.

Lily – Seven-year-old – In *The Essence of Courage* her family had decided to be the church liason for a missionary family. Lily had lots of questions about their little girl of the same age. In The Essence of Joy she has many questions about adoption.

Molly – Lily's friend. Lily's family has just adopted a little girl.

Olivia – Molly's recently adopted baby sister

Jeremy – Cinnamah-Brosia's husband – for obvious reasons he appears throughout both books.

Aaron – Cinnamah-Borsia and Jeremy's adopted son. In *The Essence of Courage* Jeremy's sister asked them to adopt Aaron, and they did. In *The Essence of Joy* Cinnamah-Brosia shares some of their adoption story with Lily.

Caryn – Jeremy and Cinnamah-Brosia's youngest child. In *The Essence of Courage* she has an opportunity to hold her best friend accountable for promises made when they were younger children. In *The Essence of Joy* she is mentioned in connection with the family's adoption story.

Amber – Molly and Oliva's mom – she answers the curious young girls' questions about adoption.

Mandy – Lily's mom – In *The Essence of Joy* she and Lily are in The Coffee Cottage and telling Cinnamah-Brosia about their new connection with a missionary family. In *The Essence of Joy* she is present during a cookie-baking day with Lily and her friends.

Molly's dad – We learn about a special gift he gave Molly, her mom, and her baby sister during the adoption.

Melanie – In *The Essence of Courage* she had been a troubled teen who remembered Miss Dot's kindness to her. In The Essence of Joy she brings up the annual gift-exchange between the members of the Tuesday night women's group meeting at The Coffee Cottage.

Carol – In *The Essence of Courage* she had a memory of Miss Dot's kindness to her when she had lost a baby. She also brought her mom (an old friend of Miss Dot's who had moved away) to The Coffee Cottage to visit. In *The Essence of Joy* she offers Haley a excellent suggestion about a gift for Cinnamah-Brosia.

Crystal – In *The Essence of Courage* we learn she's been coming to the café since she was a little girl (with her mom). She's married to Jeff and they have a little girl, Josie. In *The Essence of Joy* she's in attendance at the women's group holiday party.

Jennifer – In *The Essence of Courage* she and her husband Craig learned a big lesson while purchasing a home. In *The Essence of Joy* she's in attendance at the women's group holiday party.

Eileen – New guest at The Coffee Cottage – She shares some difficult family problems with Jane.

*Jane – In *The Essence of Courage* we meet Jane as the long-time friend of Miss Dot and Cinnamah-Brosia (and all the others). She helped in the café when it was Miss Dot's. She helps in The Coffee Cottage, too, and she leads the women's group meeting there. In *The Essence of Joy* we first meet her when she serves Eileen her beverage.

Pam – Pastor Gary's wife – She, Jane, Kaitlyn, and Cinnamah-Brosia are at The Coffee Cottage discussing some challenges following a teen star's recent concert.

Laney – Pam & Pastor Gary's twelve-year-old daughter – She didn't get to go to the recent concert.

Carson – Laney's best friend. She got involved in some trouble with drugs at the concert. Has an apology for Laney.

Carson's mom – Had encouraged Pam to take Laney to the concert. Realizes why it wasn't the best decision for any of the girls or adults to go.

Jeff – A past friend of Andy Porter's – died in an accident while driving under the influence.

Alex – Jane's husband – He introduced Jane to Jesus when she was in high school.

*Holt – In both *The Essence of Courage* and in *The Essence of Joy*, he is one of the musicians who plays on "Fish & Beans" nights.

Ashley – A very troubled high school girl from a troubled family. She reluctantly attends a "Fish & Beans" night, then chooses to trust Carol with her story.

Ryan – Ashley's brother – From the same troubled family – He's helping out at the church. Andy invited him to a special "Fish & Beans" night. He convinced his sister, Ashley, to come.

Pastor Able – An associate pastor with Pastor Gary at one of the local churches.

*Pastor Gary – In *The Essence of Courage* he was the pastor of a local church. He had officiated at Cinnamah-Brosia and Jeremy's wedding. In *The Essence of Joy* he's still the pastor. He and Pastor Able enjoy studying the Old and New Testaments together unlocking so many wonderful connections between the two.

*Star – married to Tom – In *The Essence of Courage* Star faced the deaths of her mom and her twin brother within three weeks of each other, and she experienced love and kindness from Cinnamah-Brosia that began to restore her faith. In *The Essence of Joy* we learn she and her husband Tom have been and still are raising their granddaughter, Grace. After the death of Star's mom, their wayward daughter asks for her grandmother's Bible, and a new chapter begins.

Tom – Star's husband – Tom baptizes Jessica.

Jessica – Star and Tom's daughter – she's been involved with drugs. She was very close to her grandmother and her Uncle Shane, and after their deaths she thinks about much of their encouragement toward her. Chooses to take steps to turn her life around.

Uncle Shane – Star's twin brother. He died in a motorcycle accident.

Grace – Star and Tom's ten-year-old granddaughter; Jessica's daughter.

Star's Dad – He's lonely, and Jessica needs a new and safe place to live. Her grandfather offers her a home, and they are a blessing to each other.

Star and Tom's pastor – Made the announcement that Jessica would be baptized.

*NOTE: Many of these friends were first introduced in *The Essence of Courage*. Without getting too cumbersome, we've attempted to give you a little background on each of them plus current information. The friends appearing in both books are marked by an *.

You are personally invited to join Cinnamah-Brosia and her friends throughout the year by visiting our blog: http://LynnUWatson.com/blog. Lynn posts regular updates, and you'll find a menu board there too, with links to the recipes featured at the coffee cottage.

The Pearlville Weekly   October 4, 2016

Reno Complete: Cinnamah-Brosia's Coffee Cottage & Gift Shop Open

Cinnamah-Brosia's Coffee Cottage and Gift Shop hosted a well-attended grand reopening on Saturday, October 1. The coffee cottage is the former Miss Dot's Café. Gram and "C-B's" daughter, Kaitlyn, planned the redo prior to Miss Dot's passing. The walls have been refreshed in frothy cappuccino. Regulars will remember Sophia's Corner, a favorite gathering spot at the café. With a coat of white paint, the stone fireplace is still the cottage's focal point and even more inviting. The comfort of the gingerbread leather sofa and two overstuffed turquoise chairs filled with berry-trimmed vanilla accent pillows beckon you in. Kaitlyn's creativity has turned the old round wooden coffee table into a work of art. The pomegranate border was inspired by Gram's ambrosia recipe.

The addition of a gift shop provides convenience to customers. Currently, you will find garden items, artwork, books, jewelry, and kitchen gadgets. Kaitlyn is managing the gift shop and promises to keep the inventory fresh and exciting.

Cinnamah-Brosia's name is really Cinnamon. Her Gram, Miss Dot, prayed the name as a blessing over the child when she was three years old. The suffix "ah" in Hebrew means "of God." Cinnamon representing goodness, Miss Dot reinvented the name and trusted she would witness a harvest of the goodness of God in her granddaughter's life.

Everyone who visited Miss Dot's Café remembers her ambrosia. Cinnamah-Brosia recalled, "I requested her 'brosia every day during my childhood summer visits. Ambrosia is full of fruit reminding my Gram of the fruit of the Spirit. The name is a mouthful, I know, but she put the two words together. Others found ways to shorten it, but to Gram and Gramps I was always Cinnamah-Brosia. I really do love all that it meant to them."

With the transformation come many opportunities for the people in the community to meet and hang out. The menu of scrumptious baked goods and both hot and chilled beverages guarantees a line forming every morning. The pleasant vintage space will be

available for community events in the evenings. Cinnamah-Brosia's Coffee Cottage will serve guests from 6:30 AM to 2 PM each day.
It's easy to imagine Miss Dot proudly smiling down on her granddaughter today.

NOTE: The selection above is a newspaper article (fictional, of course) that appeared as introductory material in *The Essence of Courage*. It will help new readers understand more about Cinnamah-Brosia's Coffee Cottage where she and her friends hang out.

Resources

Richard Bauckham, *Gospel Women*, (Grand Rapids, Michigan: William B. Eerdmans Publishing Company, 2002

Herbert Lockyer, *All the Women of the Bible*, (Grand Rapids, Michigan: Zondervan, 1967).

Connie and Alan Higley, *Reference Guide for Essential Oils,* (Spanish Fork, Utah: Abundant Health, 1996-2012, Thirteenth Edition revised January 2012).

Hannah Hurnard, *Mountain of Spices*, (American edition, Wheaton, Illinois: Tyndale House, 1977).

Vincenzina Krymow, *Healing Plants of the Bible: History, Lore & Meditations,* (Cincinnati, Ohio: St. Anthony Messenger Press, 2002).

John Lawton, *Silk Scents & Spice,* (Paris, France: UNESCO Publishing, 2004).

Herbert Lockyer, *All the Women of the Bible*, (Grand Rapids, Michigan: Zondervan, 1967).

Lytton John Musselman, *Figs, Dates, Laurel, and Myrrh: Plants of the Bible and the Quran,* (Portland, Oregon: Timber Press, 2007.

Ann Spangler, and Jean E. Syswerda, *Women of the Bible*, (Grand Rapids, Michigan: Zondervan, 1999).

Ann Spangler, and Jean E. Syswerda, *Women of the Bible*, (Grand Rapids, Michigan: Zondervan, 1999.

David Stewart, Ph.D., *Healing Oils of the Bible,* (Mable Hill, Missouri: Care Publications, 2003).

Allan A. Swenson, *Plants of the Bible and How to Grow Them*, (New York, New York: Kensington Publishing Corp., 1995).

OTHER:
Many websites were used to gather the information in this inspirational collection. They are included as footnotes in each chapter. All links were active at the time of publication. If link is no longer available please use your search engine to find the info on another website.

Lynn uses the Young Living™ brand of essential oils. There are other quality brands of essential oils on the market. We recommend you research the options and choose high quality oils within your budget.

Disclaimers

Cinnamah-Brosia is a fictional character. All similarities to real life people you know are totally intentional, but she is a little bit of all of us. Real women's stories were used and fictionalized (with permission) to flow with her character and the setting. We hope you found yourself and your friends right there on the coffee cottage pages. It's a great place to hang out.

Content of this book:
None of the statements in this book have been evaluated by the FDA. The information contained in this book and in any references cited is for educational and inspirational purposes only. It is not provided to diagnose, prescribe, or treat or cure any health condition. The information should not be used as a substitute for medical counseling. Caution should be exercised when using essential oils. You are responsible for educating yourself and consulting with health care professionals in any and all matters regarding the use of essential oil or other plant-based products. The author accepts no responsibility for such use. Please consult with your health care professional for all your health care needs.

Some essential oils are unsafe or should be used with great caution for children and pregnant women. Consult your medical professional before use, and educate yourself about uses and cautions.

Young Living Essential Oils™ has not endorsed any part of this book. The author is not receiving any compensation associated with this book from Young Living Essential Oils™ or any other essential oil company. No essential oil company, including but not limited to Young Living Essential Oils™, is responsible for the information in this book.

Acknowledgements

The encouragement and expertise of so many people make writing possible. I'm including a deep thank you to a few of them here. That's scary, because I'm certain I'm leaving someone out.

My husband, Steve, has once again done a great job making this book look beautiful. You continue to endure (and still love me) the adventures and misadventures of living with me. Thank you!

Allisha, you created another amazing cover illustration. Thank you for letting your light shine through your artwork.

Robin, you always find the most amazing information to inspire and encourage me as I write. Your contributions and comments are invaluable. Thank you! (…and thank you for being sure I took the bull out of the thicket. Lol)

Ashley, Charlene, Elizabeth, Gayelynn, Helen, Jan, Jeri, Rhonda, Robin, and Sherry, A warm Coffee Cottage "thank you" – stories from your life have inspired the stories of Cinnamah-Brosia and her friends. Without them there would be no Coffee Cottage where friends gather to encourage one another.

Jeanne, thank you for your continued encouragement and for taking your time to look with me at Elisheba as a pastor's wife. Your wisdom and first-hand experiences brought her to life.

My Family you inspire me everyday. Once again I've used our stories and showed God's hand in our lives. I love you all so very much.

To "The Ladies of Hope" and to each lady in my Sunday School class, thank you for your prayers and encouragement. Each one of you is a treasure.

Elizabeth, in the midst of major life changes for you, thank you for being available with your editing talents to make this book shine.

David, my favorite son, thank you for using your time and talent to create the book trailer for The Essence of Joy.

Jeri, Michelle, Pat, and Rhonda, early readers' suggestions are invaluable. Thank you for your observations and suggestions bringing greater clarity and meaning to the devotions. You accomplished this in a very short time, and I am grateful. Hugs for your most kind words of praise for *The Essence of Joy*.

To God be all the glory . . .

Dear Friends,

Merry Christmas! Happy Holidays! Joyous Celebrations, Everyone!

We met some of you with the release of *The Essence of Courage*. Welcome back! Many of you are our brand new friends. Welcome! We love that our Coffee Cottage family is growing.

We've shared more of our stories, and you've met more of our friends. Would you introduce yourselves to us, too? Remember to share your own stories. Below you will find the links to our Facebook page and our website. Come, hang out with us.

We've planned one more inspirational volume in this collection: *The Essence of Love*. We'll be looking at 1 Corinthians 13, and the marriage feast that the Father and Jesus are preparing for us. Read through the 'Love' chapter again. What comes to your mind from your own stories of love? When you join our mailing list, you will receive calls for stories. We would love to include yours – ficitionalized, of course, just as all the Cinnamah-Brosia and Friends stories have been in the volume and the last one.

The door at The Coffee Cottage is open. Come on in. Share a cup of coffee and lots of Jesus!

Hugs,

Cinnamah-Brosia

> *Send forth Your light and Your truth— let them guide me. Let them bring me to Your holy mountain and to Your dwelling places. Then I will come to the altar of God, to the God of my exceeding joy, —O God, my God.*
>
> ~Psalm 43:3-4 (TLV)

http://LynnUWatson.com
http://Facebook.com/lynnuwatsonwriter

The Collection to Date:

Cinnamah-Brosia's Inspirational Collection for Women: Volume 1

The Essence of Courage

**Cultivating the Fruit of the Spirit
in Solomon's Locked Garden and in Your Heart**

Cinnamah-Brosia's Inspirational Collection for Women: Volume 2

The Essence of Joy:

Filling Your Heart with the Aromas of Jesus' Nativity

Coming in 2018:

Cinnamah-Brosia's Inspirational Collection for Women: Volume 3

The Essence of Love

About the Author:

Lynn Watson combines many years' experience in women's ministry, love of essential oils, and her passion for God's word to bring her readers freshly inspired encouragement for their walk with Jesus. Her devotional, The Essence of Courage, was recognized as a 'must read' by regional publishing industry leaders. Married since 1973, Lynn and Steve have filled their Bartlett, Tennessee home with handmade treasures and lots of love for family, especially their five beautiful (of course) grandchildren. Aromas of freshly baked bread often fill Lynn's kitchen. Jasmine, her tuxedo kitty, enjoys sleeping in Lynn's lap while she writes.

www.ingramcontent.com/pod-product-compliance
Lightning Source LLC
Chambersburg PA
CBHW071921290426
44110CB00013B/1430